W. R. Trivett,
Appalachian Pictureman

To Mother
Susie Guy Trivett

W. R. TRIVETT,
Appalachian Pictureman

PHOTOGRAPHS OF
A BYGONE TIME

by
Ralph E. Lentz II

CONTRIBUTIONS TO SOUTHERN APPALACHIAN STUDIES, 4

McFarland & Company, Inc., Publishers
Jefferson, North Carolina, and London

Library of Congress Cataloguing-in-Publication Data

Lentz, Ralph E., 1972–
    W. R. Trivett, Appalachian pictureman : photographs of a bygone
time / by Ralph E. Lentz II.
        p.   cm. – (Contributions to southern Appalachian studies ; 4)
    Includes bibliographical references and index.
    ISBN 0-7864-0927-4 (softcover : 55# finch opaque paper) ∞
    1. Trivett, W.R. (Willie Roby), 1884-1966. 2. Photographers–
Appalachian Region, Southern–Biography. 3. Photographers–
North Carolina–Biography 4. Portrait photography–Appalachian
Region, Southern. 5. Portrait photography–North Carolina.
6. Appalachian Region, Southern–Pictorial works. I. Trivett, W.R.
(Willie Roby), 1884-1966. II. Title III. Series.
TR140.T75L46 2001
770'.92—dc21
[B]   00-48956

British Library cataloguing data are available

Front cover: Original Trivett print (*background*; cars on Beech
Mountain); *back*: W.R. Trivett and Haskell Trivett making pictures
on Highway 67 at the Butler bridge, Tennessee, July 31, 1949.

Manufactured in the United States of America

McFarland & Company, Inc., Publishers
  Box 611, Jefferson, North Carolina 28640
  · *www.mcfarlandpub.com*

Acknowledgments

I am the vine, you are the branches ... without Me you can do nothing. John 15:5

Many people have encouraged and aided me in undertaking this study of the life and photographs of W. R. Trivett. They have made it an enriching experience and a labor of love.

First thanks must go to my grandmother, Susie Guy Trivett, who gave me full access to Willie's negatives and papers; her memories of Willie, Mertie, and Haskell Trivett have kept them alive in my imagination. Through her I have known Willie. Mother was also instrumental in identifying many of the people in the pictures.

Second, this book would never have seen the light of day had it not been for the patience, expertise, and generosity of my friend, mentor, and hero William (Bill) Barrett, Sr., who printed all of Willie's negatives. I know that Willie would be proud to see how beautiful his photographs look over 70 years after he first crystallized the images presented in this work.

Ottie Greene, Auborn Trivett, and Viola Ward Guy took me into their homes and provided invaluable information about W. R. Trivett and the times in which he lived. Special thanks to Melvin and Regina Jones, who provided the minute books to the Flat Springs Baptist Church. I have always felt at home there. Erleen McGuire Church helped to identify many of the people in the photographs, and is an eminent historian concerning the Dark Ridge and Flat Springs communities. William Foster Norris took me one Sunday evening to see Carl Edmisten's son, Paul, who helped identify some of the people in the pictures. I had a wonderful time watching those two reminisce about younger days in the mountains as they pored over photos of their pals. Harvey Trivett, Willie's nephew, also encouraged me in my work. Sana Ross Gaffney taught me the meaning of serendipity, and is a better connection than the Internet.

On 20 September 1997, at the Cove Creek Farm Heritage Days, Peggy and Hugh Hagaman identified Susie Hagaman Trivette (holding the baby in plate 1), mother of a future vice-chancellor of Appalachian State University—Ned Trivette. Two years later in December 1999, I spent a very pleasant afternoon with Ned and his delightful sister Mary Faye (Trivette) Tester (the baby in Susie Trivette's arms in plate 1) looking at Willie's pictures and discussing mutual family connections. They provided further information about their mother that proved very helpful, and were extremely encouraging and excited about bringing this history to life.

Several people at Appalachian State University contributed to this study as well. I am honored to have had the counsel of Dr. John A. Williams (my mentor in graduate school), Dr. Lynne M. Getz, and Dr. Charles A. Watkins. Dr. Watkins was an immense help in interpreting the work of the picturemen, and from the very beginning encouraged me to make this study more than just a picture book. The chairperson of the History Department, Dr. Michael G. Wade, helped to get money to pay for the printing of the negatives, and also provided records of the National Youth Administration in North Carolina. His support and encouragement are very much appreciated. Evelyn Shepherd, retired secretary of the History Department, also took much interest in this project and suggested several people and sources that were very helpful.

The staff of Belk Library deserves much credit for the successful completion of this work. John Heaton introduced me to Bessie Willis Hoyt's *Come When the Timber Turns*, which became a rich source for much of this book. Dean Williams of the Appalachian Collection at Belk Library also pointed out other helpful sources.

I wish also to thank Jerry Cotten, head of the Photographic Services Section at Wilson Library, UNC–Chapel Hill, for permission to use two of Bayard Wootten's photographs in this study. Likewise, I also thank Dr. Robert Boyce, chairperson of Berea College's Art Department, and the Doris Ulmann Foundation for permission to use two Doris Ulmann prints in the third chapter.

Staff members of the Watauga County Register of Deeds were especially courteous and helpful, as were Tammy Baker and Michelle Clawson at the Avery County Register of Deeds. Special thanks to Ruth Edmisten Lentz (Mama Ruth) for permission to use the portrait of her parents in Chapter II.

Kurt and Nancy Guy, Deloris Lentz, Linda and Carroll Clawson, Ethel Clawson, and Vernon Guy devoted much time to identifying the photographs, and to sharing their memories of Willie, Mertie, and Haskell Trivett.

Indeed, this work is in many ways my attempt to capture the magic of a lifetime of Sundays at Mother's reliving the past and getting to know wonderful people whom I never met—but did know. The Guys, Clawsons, and Lentzs have been a faithful bulwark of support from the beginning, and it is with great pleasure that I thank them all.

Finally, thanks to Dad and Mom—for 28 years of support and love.

Ralph E. Lentz II
Blowing Rock, NC
Fall 2000

Contents

Introduction

For the most part, the popular perception of the Appalachian region has been formed through the words and pictures of authors and photographers who were only sojourners in the mountains. In the early 1930s photographers such as Doris Ulmann and Bayard Wootten flitted into the mountains of western North Carolina, made highly sophisticated, contrived, images of the mountain people, and then returned to New York and Chapel Hill to publish their photographs. Their images were works of art—artifice—that were taken as objective reality. Yet long before urban photographic artists "discovered" Appalachia in the 1930s, mountain people's portraits were being taken by an obscure group of indigenous, self-taught professional photographers known as "picturemen." The picturemen's work was perhaps no less contrived than that of outside photographers who came to the mountains, but with the picturemen it was the mountain people who were in control of the contriving.

Willie Roby Trivett (1884–1966), a native of Watauga County in western North Carolina whose primary vocation was farming, was one such pictureman. He lived his adult life in the Beech Mountain community of neighboring Avery County, and from 1907 through the late 1940s supplemented his income by making portraits of his fellow residents and their families. The life and photographs of W. R. Trivett present an excellent opportunity to carefully examine and evaluate the work of the Appalachian picturemen. By answering the questions as to why and how Trivett made his pictures, and by placing his work within the context of the times in which they were made, the value of his and other picturemen's often neglected or trivialized images reveals itself. And what is found within the photographs of W. R. Trivett is a quiet revelation about life in Appalachia.

1

About the Photographs

W. R. Trivett's negatives (and a large collection of his extant original prints) came providentially to me through my grandmother, Susie Guy Trivett. My grandmother married Haskell Trivett in the early 1960s, and they lived together with Willie and Mertie in their Flat Springs home. Willie's negatives were stored in his "picture house" and the loft of the woodshed adjacent to his home. During 1996 and 1997, William (Bill) Barrett, a dear friend and professional photographer who resides in Sugar Grove, NC—not far from where Willie grew up—made original prints from all of Willie's surviving negatives. The negatives were "contact printed," a process whereby the negative is laid directly on the photographic paper, and is not enlarged or reduced in any way. Thus a 5 × 7 negative printed in this manner produces a 5 × 7 print. This is the same method of printing that Willie used himself. Unless otherwise noted in the photographic captions, all of Willie's photographs have been reproduced in their original size.

Chapter I

Willie

The death of W. R. Trivett on August 3, 1966, occasioned little more than nine lines in Avery County's only newspaper, *The Avery Journal*:

> Willie R. Trivett,[1] 81, of Elk Park, Rt. 1, was dead on arrival at a Marion Hospital last Wednesday night after suffering a heart attack. Mr. Trivett was a native of Watauga County and a retired farmer. Surviving are the widow...[2]

Perhaps such is befitting a retired farmer from an obscure county of western North Carolina. Yet W. R. Trivett's life, when examined, is much less prosaic than his obituary. The obituary, for instance, did not mention his life as a carpenter, a sheriff's deputy, or local dentist (or at least as a tooth-puller).[3] Most significantly, it failed to mention more than 400 glass plate negatives of photographs taken between 1907 and the late 1940s in rural Avery and Watauga counties which Trivett had produced as a self-taught professional photographer. These remain as W. R. Trivett's greatest legacy, and are the primary inspiration for this history.

Along with his photographs, however, Trivett also left behind a small cache of papers which provide rich, if fragmented, details about his life. For this the historian must give thanks to Mertie Weaver Trivett, W. R.'s wife. Over the 59 years of their marriage, Mertie Trivett saved some of the most trivial—and important—artifacts of her and her husband's life: postcards penned with lines of love, old paycheck stubs, tax records, correspondence from childhood friends and family; solicitations from mail order companies, one of her diminutive calling cards, one of W. R. Trivett's business cards; her grandfather's notebooks from his country store which date back to the 1890s.

Many of the items, such as the romantic post cards, were no doubt reminders of precious feelings and times. At any rate, articles both precious and mundane were kept in an old trunk and passed down to W. R. Trivett's daughter-in-law, Susie Guy Trivett, in whose possession they remain to this day. These papers provide a glimpse of the shadow of W. R. Trivett and the times in which he lived. And by examining his life, along with his photographs (which will be considered in the following chapters), another view—a different view—of Appalachia presents itself.

Childhood

There are no records of W. R. Trivett's childhood among his personal papers, and the details of his early youth remain the secrets of the mountains, fields, and creek banks where he played. However, his family lineage is readily available through census reports and birth and death certificates. And while there exist no report cards from his days in school, enough has been written about the development of education in Watauga County to provide a composite sketch of what his education might have been like.

W. R. Trivett's father, Goulder C. Trivett (1856–1935), was born in the Laurel Creek township of Watauga County, and was the oldest of seven children.[4] Like most other residents of Watauga County, he made his living as a farmer.[5] In 1881 Goulder Trivett married Martha Harmon (1864–1940). While residing in Laurel Creek township they had 11 children, although one died either at birth or in infancy.[6] Willie Roby Trivett was the second oldest child, born on October 27, 1884. He had six brothers—Andrew, David, Council, Clark, McKinley, and Henry L.—and three sisters: Mary E., Vada C., and Epsy E. Trivett.[7]

It is known from an interview with his nephew that W. R. Trivett received his education at the Windy Gap School, located only a mile from his parents' home in the Laurel Creek township.[8] How long he attended is unknown, but he was among the minority of children who went to school in Watauga County during the late 19th and early 20th centuries. In 1900, of 5,050 white children of school age, 3,794 were enrolled in school. Those who actually attended averaged 2,101, or about 41 percent.[9]

Yet there was no dearth of educational opportunity in the Watauga County of W. R. Trivett's youth. In compliance with the 1869 North Carolina School Law, Watauga County was divided into school districts—each district not to exceed an area of six square miles. By the turn of the 19th

PLATE 1. ORIGINAL W.R.T. PRINT 5" × 7"

Taken in the summer of 1929 in the Sugar Grove area of Watauga County. Susie Hagaman Trivette, mother of a future vice-chancellor of Appalachian State University—Ned Trivette—can be seen in the second row, second from the left, with glasses (holding Ned's sister, Mary Faye).

century the county had 71 school districts, with a total of 72 one room school houses (one district had two schools in it).[10] Three of these schools served the county's black population. In Laurel Creek schools abounded; besides Windy Gap School, in 1886 the Presnell School was formed. Three years later the Rominger School opened, and in 1895 the Johnson School opened near the Watauga River.[11] Still, lack of good roads and means of transporting the children to school, poverty, and apathy combined to keep many of the county's children outside the pale of education. As one Avery County woman wrote, "I never went to school but little as it was so far and not very good clothes to wear."[12]

During the time when Trivett most likely attended school, from 1890 through 1904, the majority of the county's schools were log structures, although there were some frame buildings as well.[13] William J. Farthing, a student and teacher in Watauga County schools from 1873 through 1900, described the school houses as being "built about twenty feet by thirty feet with a large chimney at each end."[14] The boys, he recalled, were responsible for getting wood for the fireplace at noon recess. Teaching equipment was sparse. Students sat on homemade benches and did their lessons with a soap-stone pencil on a piece of slate about the size of a piece of typing paper.[15] Before the turn of the 19th century desks were nonexistent. Heat was provided by either a fireplace or a cast-iron wood burning stove.

In 1898 the school year in Watauga County lasted 55 days.[16] During this time one teacher could expect to teach around 28 pupils, from ages 6 to 20.[17] Records kept by the Watauga County superintendent of education in 1890 show that most of the county's scholars were young—229 were six years old, 199 were seven, 196 were eight, 224 were nine, 228 were ten, 215 were eleven, and 217 were twelve.[18] In 1890 831 of the county's students studied arithmetic; 392 geography; 357 English grammar; 54 were engaged in studying North Carolina history; 65 in United States history; and 57 in physiology and hygiene.[19] Trivett and other children attending school in Watauga County were exposed to such textbooks as *Sanford's Arithmetic*, *Harvey's Grammar*, *Holmes' Readers*, *Morris' Geography*, and *Mon's Histories*.[20] There were neither grades nor division of students by age in the county's schools; rather, students advanced by completing books.[21]

Judging from Trivett's letters, it is apparent that penmanship, spelling, and grammar were not his long suits. Yet clearly he was competent in basic arithmetic: a notebook dating from 1915 shows that he kept a record of the people for whom he made pictures and the prices he charged. In sum, it is safe to say that Trivett received a practical education, and that he enjoyed the benefits thereof.

Young Adulthood—Making a Living

Opportunities for making a living in rural Watauga County at the turn of the century were largely limited to harvesting the resources of the land. Besides farming, many supplemented their incomes by gathering herbs and bark. Galax, "dog hobble," wild fern, ginseng, and "may apple" were all purchased by wholesalers in the county seat of Boone. No one ever got rich picking galax; it sold for fifty cents a thousand, and had to be bunched in groups of 25 leaves.[22]

Like many other sons and daughters of Appalachia, by the 1920s some in Watauga and Avery counties went north to work in the factories of Detroit, Akron, and New York.[23] Many worked just to get enough cash to sustain their families for half a year, and then returned home. Others left and came back to the mountains only to retire. To the west in Elizabethton, Tennessee, one could find work in the rayon mills, and to the east the furniture and textile mills of the Carolina piedmont offered steady employment.

Leaving the mountains of his youth for work in a factory did not appeal to Trivett. He did try some mill work—saw milling to be specific; through 1906 and 1907 Trivett worked intermittently with the W. M. Ritter Lumber Company.[24] Apparently he did not find work at the lumber mill too enjoyable, and two pay envelopes found among his papers perhaps reveal why. In February 1906 Trivett earned 75 cents, and another undated pay envelope shows that he earned $1.90. In May 1907, Trivett worked 156 hours at the company's Pineola saw mill, earning a gross pay of $23.40. However, $9.50 in deductions—$9.00 spent at the company store and 50 cents for a visit to the doctor—left him a net pay of $13.90.[25] Saw milling was dangerous, back-breaking, ear-splitting work that did not pay well. Thus at the age of 26 and living at home with his parents, W. R. Trivett's occupation was listed in the 1910 census of Watauga County as "farm laborer." Ten years later, married, with wife, son, and one hired servant, and living in the Flat Springs community in the Beech Mountain township of Avery County, Trivett's occupation was still listed in the 1920 census as "farmer."[26] Farming remained the primary source of his sustenance for the rest of his life, though interviews with his daughter-in-law, a nephew, and a close friend of his son reveal that Trivett also worked as a carpenter, and occasional dentist.[27] In this last capacity, however, he had no professional training, and apparently only did it as a community service, rather than as a means of making a living. The other great work of his life—photography—will be examined in depth in the following chapter.

Three articles in Trivett's papers dating from the 1930s indicate his role as a respected and active leader of the Flat Springs community. The first article, a paper dated December 3, 1934, and signed by Avery County Sheriff W. H. Hughes, documents Trivett's appointment as a deputy sheriff.[28] The other two articles reveal Trivett and his son's involvement in the National Youth Administration during the Great Depression. According to the NYA unit and project time report found in Trivett's papers, he served as the supervisor for Ellen Stout of Whaley, North Carolina, on NYA project number 1-10613 from November 8 through November 22, 1937.[29] What this specific project entailed remains a mystery, for there is no mention of it in either of the two local newspapers of the day, the *Watauga Democrat* or *Avery Advocate*. Later, in July 1940, a postcard sent from the Avery County NYA supervisor to Trivett's son, Haskell, shows that he also found employment on a NYA project at the Whaley school building.[30] The National Youth Administration's work in Watauga and Avery counties, despite its merit and importance, has been examined but little; a brief survey of its history in western North Carolina can shed some light on W. R. Trivett and his son's life during the Great Depression.

In 1935, one-sixth of the nation's population was between the ages of 16 and 24, and the Great Depression had made this generation's prospects for employment just as bad as (if not worse than) those of their parents.[31] With some 4 million restless, unemployed, untrained youth with time to kill on their hands, the Roosevelt administration felt the need to provide relief for this beleaguered segment of the population. On June 26, 1935, Franklin D. Roosevelt created by Executive Order No. 7086 the National Youth Administration as a division of the Works Progress Administration. The NYA had four main objectives: first, to provide money for the part-time employment of needy high school, college, and graduate students between the ages of 16 and 25, so that they could continue their education; second, to fund work projects to provide part-time employment for 18 to 25 year olds of relief family status; third, to foster the establishment of job training, counseling, and placement services for youth; and fourth, "to encourage the development and extension of instructive leisure time activities."[32]

Because of North Carolina's large rural youth population, particularly in the mountains, the NYA was especially active in the western portion of the state during its eight year history.[33] In its first two years of operation, the NYA employed mountain youths in "privy" construction and other community sanitation projects, library book repair, janitorial work in public buildings, clerical work assistance in government offices, and supplemental work in the statewide WPA recreation projects.[34] From 1937 on, the emphasis of NYA activities in Watauga and Avery counties was placed on the production of various crafts. Four NYA craft shops in Watauga County provided vocational training and produced furniture—"both rustic and domestic" (which was put to good use in the public waiting room of the welfare office in the Watauga courthouse)—as well as pottery and hooked, braided and punched rugs.[35] In Avery County one "social and recreational building" was erected by the NYA.[36] Perhaps W. R. Trivett's son, Haskell, participated in its building when he was employed by the NYA in July 1940.[37]

W. R. Trivett contentedly settled down to farming for the majority of his adult life. Yet some interesting articles found among his personal papers suggest that as a young man he considered the possibilities of working in the wide world outside of Watauga and Avery counties. And employment opportunities from the outside world came early to him via the U.S. Mail.

In May 1905, Trivett received solicitation for a job as a sales agent for the World Bible House mail-order company of Philadelphia. Established in 1893, and boasting $100,000 in capital, the World Bible House Company offered

> hundreds of miscellaneous books, Bibles and albums.... Solid Alaska Silver Table Ware, Roger's Triple plated Flat Ware and Quadruple Plated Hollow Ware, Celluloid Novelties, Fountain Pens, Games, Toys, Puzzles, and hundreds of Household Necessities.[38]

The money was seemingly good—a salary of $2.50 per day, with no outlay of capital or sales experience required. Yet in the salary contract enclosed in the literature sent to Trivett, it was apparent that it was not necessarily easy money to be made. The contract stipulated that the sales agent was responsible for "carefully studying and committing to memory all" instructions and literature sent with the sales merchandise.[39] It was also the agent's duty to thoroughly canvass the territory assigned to him (or her) by the company, and to make weekly written reports about their sales activities which the company would examine periodically. Delivery of the merchandise to subscribers and the remittance of the retail price back to the company were also among the sales agent's responsibilities. Sixty days was the minimum contract length. In the business letter addressed to Trivett, company president Geo. A. Parker assured him that the products of the World Bible House "go with everybody."[40] Teachers, ministers in failing health or retired from active service, students, women, farmers and farmers' sons could, according to Geo. A Parker, with a "moderate share of Pluck and Push ... readily clear from $100 to $250 per month from the start."[41] Yet, for whatever reasons, Trivett did not further pursue the opportunity to become a World Bible House sales agent; the salary contract remained unsigned and was found among his papers 91 years later.

Once again in the summer of 1909, correspondence from the business world presented Trivett with a way out of Watauga County and a life of tilling the soil. This time the call came in the form of "Dots and Dashes," a flier published quarterly by the Southern School of Telegraphy of Newnan, Georgia.

> Don't you have enough self-confidence to believe that you are worthy
> of easier and pleasanter work, a larger monthly salary, a position that
> offers promotion in proportion to one's ability, and loyalty to the ser-
> vice wherein one is employed?[42]

The answer, of course, was "yes," and telegraphy—more specifically
the Southern School of Telegraphy—was the means to the end. Starting pay
for telegraphers in 1909 (according to the author of "Dots and Dashes")
was between $45 to $60 per month, with "limitless" chances of promotion.
Such a lucrative salary could be obtained after only five months of instruction in telegraphy. Tuition to the school was $50, with "good board and
home-like accommodations" costing $10 to $12 per month.[43] The total cost
came to $113.40, an amount which Trivett may have found out of his reach.
At any rate, telegraphy did not become a part of his future, and helping
his father farm remained W. R. Trivett's chief occupation for at least the
next year.

If the chance of rapid financial improvement did not appeal to Trivett
in the form of becoming a sales agent or as a telegraph operator, the opportunity to improve his penmanship did. In the fall of 1909, Trivett wrote a
letter to the Ransomerian School of Penmanship of Kansas City, Missouri,
inquiring about their correspondence course in penmanship. By December
he received a two page letter (typed) from C. W. Ransom, president and
manager of the school, detailing the benefits of aesthetically pleasing writing. According to Ransom, those with good penmanship skills were very
much in demand as teachers of penmanship at business colleges, as book-
keepers, clerks, and stenographers. "Not only is it a necessity in business,"
stated Ransom, "but it is a source of great satisfaction in a social way."[44]
The Ransomerian method of writing consisted of 82 one week lessons in
business and ornamental writing, pen lettering, designing, engrossing, and
card writing, as well as optional courses in "double entry bookkeeping"
and shorthand.[45] The cost of the course was $30, payable in six monthly
installments of $5 each.

Scattered intermittently among Trivett's papers is evidence that he
practiced the Ransomerian method of writing somewhat—there are pieces
of paper where he wrote his name several times in a flowery, cursive manner. Though his penmanship would have certainly benefited from instruction, perhaps because of financial considerations, Trivett never signed the
application for enrollment sent to him by Ransom.

Like many young people first trying to make their own way in life,
W. R. Trivett for a time looked beyond the confines of his home to the

larger world outside of Avery and Watauga counties. Yet the contact Trivett had with the metropolitan world of professional sales agents, the modern communications industry, and correspondence education never pulled him away from the plow. One aspect of the outside world which he came into contact with through the mail did capture his imagination, however, and became a major facet of his life—photography. But there is more to life than just making a living, and W. R. Trivett as a young man also pursued a companion to share his life with. The record of this pursuit—or at least a partial record—is found among postcards and letters saved by Trivett and his wife. When examined, they add color and vitality to the portrait of this mild man.

Mertie

...oh Merte it made me feel bad for you to rite like i doand [sic] care anything for you. i cant think any more of you and i do for i Love you as i due my sefe and you no this Love and Every word of this is so ... my Love is all yours and no other one. this from your Loven sweet harth.

Willie Trivett[46]

W. R. Trivett wrote these lines in April 1911. The object of his affection was a young lady named Mertie Weaver. Her parents were Hiram "Lucky" Weaver (1866–1936) and Sallie J. Harmon (1871–1942), both of whom resided in the Laurel Creek area of Watauga County. They later moved to Tennessee. While living in North Carolina, Hiram Weaver farmed, and his wife oversaw the raising of ten children, of which Mertie Weaver (1890–1976) was the oldest. She had two sisters—Hessie N. and Daisy, and six brothers—Bynum H., James A., Thomas (Tom), Smith, Grady, and Ted H. (Apparently one of her siblings had died prior to the 1910 census.)[47]

Judging from correspondence sent to her, and from her own letters, Mertie Weaver was an educated and avid reader and letter writer. She often quoted poems and songs in her letters, and she exchanged copies of songs with her cousin Ethel Weaver of East Bend, North Carolina (near Winston-Salem).[48] "Marching Through Georgia," a Civil War era song, and the bittersweet ballad "Juanita" are among the songs copied by Weaver. More interesting is a segment from "The Ten Famous Women," found among her letters. The portion copied by Weaver contains a reference to England's Queen Victoria, and encapsulates the Victorian code of the ideal woman—

Young lovers—Mertie Weaver and W. R. Trivett, ca. 1911. This photograph may have been to commemorate Trivett and Weaver's engagement.

The Trivett family, ca. 1919: Mertie, W. R., and Haskell. This is one of Trivett's few self-portraits. Mertie remained one of his favorite subjects throughout his career as a photographer. The photos on the following pages are some of Trivett's original prints of his beloved wife taken over their years together.

a code which Weaver, and many of her generation, believed, at least prior to the 1920s. The poem stated:

> All men say that woman cannot rule, that hers is only to obey; But unto thee men bend the knee, and England owned thy regal sway.... With reason firm, and temperance wise, Endurance, foresight, strength, skill—A perfect woman, nobly planned to warm, to comfort, and command; all Blessing she was; God made her so, and deeds of weekday holiness fell from her, miseless [sic] as the snow, For did she ever chance to know that aught were easier than to bless.[49]

This is one of the earliest photographs of Mertie Weaver taken by W. R. Trivett in the early 1900s. The two young adults standing are, left to right, Mertie Weaver and Rebecca Harmon. The little girl is listed as "Clois."

Continuing, the poem admonished women to do their work "well, Be brave and pure and good, and great or small your part in life, Hold fast your womanhood." In "Charity," an allegory partially copied by Weaver, the angelic nature ascribed to women in Victorian culture is even more explicitly expressed. Pledged to watch over their fallen and imprisoned brother (mankind), three angelic sisters state their mission:

> Heaven help us then; thou sweet hope, shall be my guiding star; and thou, dear faith, my anchor; and mine shall be the hand to lift our fallen brother, and save him from ruin ... we are sisters to all mankind. There is none so low as to be beneath our notice, and none so degraded as to deserve our scorn. When a poor erring mortal has advanced far down the broad road to ruin, and a world joins its forces to dash him over the brink of destruction, then it is our mission to win him back, set him on an equal footing with us, and teach him the way to Heaven.[50]

That Mertie Weaver Trivett subscribed to the Victorian concept of womanhood is evident in her letters. This is not to say that she practiced them all (and no mortal could). Like some other middle and upper class women of Gilded Age America, Mertie Trivett suffered from "the hypo"— abnormal worry over imagined or otherwise nonthreatening illnesses. In her later years she was annually bedridden for the duration of winter. Those who knew her have speculated that depression was the primary cause of her self-imposed exile to the bedroom.[51]

The record of W. R. Trivett's courtship of Mertie Weaver dates to a postcard of March 17, 1908, apparently sent by a coquettish Weaver. Written on the front of the postcard are the words "apple pie without cheese is like a kiss without a squeeze." On the back Mertie teased Trivett with these lines: "go go I said to my love" (the postcard featured a picture of "Old Frisco" [San Francisco]), and "when you are married and living in the west, Remember I'm single and courting my best, from a friend, guess who." Over the course of the next five years Trivett and Weaver spent most of their Sundays together courting.[52] Their relationship blossomed early, and Weaver wrote more than once in the same vein as these lines from a 1909 letter to Trivett:

Mertie, 1920

> green grows the willow
> yellow grows the Bark
> others have my friend
> ship But you have
> my heart good Bye
> Sweet heart
> But I hope not for
> Ever darling Willie[53]

There were others who for a time caught Trivett's fancy, but Mertie Weaver remained his "best girl."[54] The culmination of the romance came on December 25, 1913, when the two betrothed each other's lives to one another as a Christmas present.[55] From all accounts theirs was a long and happy marriage, which ended only with the death of W. R. Trivett in 1966. The couple was blessed with one son, Haskell Bynum Trivett (1918–1988).

While growing up Mertie Weaver apparently spent much time with her maternal grandparents, William Mathias ("Tice") (1845–1928) and

Mertie Weaver

Elizabeth Harmon (1848–1936), of the Beech Mountain township of Avery County.[56] Her relationship with her grandparents was warm; she was referred to in the Harmons' 1927 will as "our beloved Grand Daughter."[57] William Harmon was a dry goods merchant whose store in the Flat Springs community of Beech Mountain township was evidently fairly prosperous.[58] He kept detailed records of his business dating back to 1896, and they along with other miscellaneous papers show that he sold tools, flour, corn, fertilizers, paint, machine oils, books, and a host of patent medicines up until 1926.[59] Moreover, Harmon was a Mason (of the Hall of Snow, Lodge 363), and a student of the Beery Correspondence School of Horsemanship of Pleasant Hill, Ohio.[60] He owned a considerable amount of land in the Flat Springs community—at least 77 acres—and his notebooks show that he loaned money to many people in the area.[61]

In fact, it was William and Elizabeth Harmon who enabled W. R. and Mertie Trivett to settle in the Flat Springs community. After their marriage in December 1913, the Trivetts spent four years in somewhat of a transitory existence, living for a time in Butler, Tennessee, and various other places around Flat Springs.[62] In the summer of 1917, however, W. R. Trivett paid $255 to the Harmons for 36 acres of land in the heart of the Flat Springs community.[63] Nine years later, in October 1926, W. R. and Mertie Trivett paid the Harmons $1,000 for an

Mertie, ca. 1932

additional 40 acres of land (which included the Harmons' house) adjoining their first tract of property. The health of the Harmons was steadily declining by this time, and the deed reveals that the Trivetts at this point moved into the Harmons' house to take care of them.[64] The Harmons' two-story, three bedroom frame house remained W. R., Mertie, and Haskell Trivett's home for the rest of their lives.

Brother Willie Trivett

In W. R. Trivett's day and community, the church universal was the Southern Baptist. The Bible was taken literally as the word of God. Sin, humanity's depravity, and the need for repentance and redemption through the sacrificial blood of Jesus Christ were the cornerstones of the church's doctrine. Jonathan Edwards' "Sinners in the Hands of an Angry God," if not delivered verbatim, was preached in spirit by the mountain ministers.[65]

Mertie, 1942

For Trivett, the church was the central institution in his life. And it is Trivett's spiritual life—perhaps the most elusive and unknowable aspect of any person's existence in this world—that is the most thoroughly documented.

On Saturday, January 27, 1923, Trivett and his wife joined by letter the Flat Springs Baptist Church of Christ of Avery County, North Carolina.[66] From that time forward, Trivett's role in the church was meticulously recorded in the minute books of the church, which date from September 1902 to the present. In interviews with Trivett's daughter-in-law, his nephew, and his son's best friend, the most singular memory they had of him was his devotion to the church.[67] The minutes of the Flat Springs Baptist Church of Christ thoroughly substantiate these recollections, and reveal more about Trivett's character than any other source.

Formed on September 20, 1902, by 17 Christians (nine females and eight males), the Flat Springs Baptist Church of Christ wrestled mightily with the sins of its brothers and sisters during the first 37 years of its existence.[68] During this time the church's minutes are largely devoted to recording the spiritual falls and stumblings of its members; on several occasions members were cited for "herisy" (heresy), for "swaring," for nonattendance and or not answering the call of the church, for public "drunkness," for "disorderly walking," for fornication and adultery, for giving birth to "a base-born" child, and for card playing.[69] The ultimate reprimand from the church was to "withdraw fellowship" from the offending member, and this happened frequently. However, also recorded are instances where repentant members publicly acknowledged their sin and were forgiven by the church and restored to full fellowship.[70]

On October 27, 1927, Trivett and his wife were given a letter of dismission, apparently to join another church. Yet by November 1929, Trivett appeared again in the church's chronicles, and the record of his service in the church continued unbroken until July 11, 1964—only two years before his death. The standard badges of church involvement are all there: on July 16, 1932, Trivett was elected church sexton; on May 20, 1933, he became a deacon; on March 3, 1935, his son Haskell was baptized; in 1937 he was appointed Sunday School superintendent; in 1936, 1940, 1943, 1947, 1952, and 1956 he was delegate to the meeting of the Avery County Baptist Association.[71]

More revealing of the personal commitment to his faith, however, are the church minutes which record Trivett's service on committees sent to reconcile wayward members. Many times throughout his membership with the church, Trivett was appointed with other members to counsel fallen brothers and sisters for swearing,

Original W. R. Trivett print of Mertie Trivett, ca. 1932.

public drunkenness, or various other sins. The first time Trivett served on such a committee came in June 1922, when he, along with J. M. Greene and Roy Guy, were appointed to see two other members charged with swearing and "drunkness." On 16 July 1932, Trivett and the rest of the "committee" gave a report to the church of their meeting with the offending members; apparently the wayward brothers were unrepentant—fellowship was withdrawn from them the same day.[72] It is likely today that

W. R. Trivett, 1884–1966

this would be interpreted by nonbelievers (and many Christians as well) to be no more than the nosy meddling of self-righteous busy-bodies, but it is more indicative of traditional Baptist doctrine and of the Christian's concern and love for the welfare of their brethren's soul. This is nowhere better illustrated than in W. R. Trivett's advocacy for Eugene Guy.[73]

In the late summer of 1945, Eugene Guy stumbled some way in the faith (his offense is not specifically recorded), and Trivett was appointed to talk with him concerning the matter in September. Guy's case lingered into December, and on the 22nd of that month Trivett made his report to the church. After having talked with both Guy and his wife, Trivett appealed to the church not to withdraw fellowship from him, and a motion was made (possibly by Trivett) to give Guy another month to make his acknowledgment and confession before the church.[74] At the next meeting of the church, Trivett again appealed for grace concerning Guy, stating that "he thought that the church ought not to withdraw fellowship" from him.[75] On Sunday, January 27, 1946, Trivett's pleas for mercy came to fruition—Guy came before the church for prayer, stated that "the Lord had forgiven him," and then asked for the church's forgiveness. Guy's transgression was forgiven, "and the church [gave] him their hand."[76] It is notable that in 64 years of recorded history at Flat Springs Baptist Church, (1902–1966), W. R. Trivett was the only member ever cited to come before the church on behalf of an indicted fellow worshipper.[77]

*   *   *

The papers of W. R. Trivett provide a partial portrait of the man and the times in which he lived. They reveal a mountain man who was not ignorant of the modern world, nor untouched by its influences—whether it be through the availability of mass produced goods sold by mail-order companies, or the dearth of employment caused by the Great Depression. W. R. Trivett was educated, though not eloquent; he was a community leader, but not elite; he lived a quiet, but not uneventful life. Like most other men in his community, he pursued the vocation of working the land to support himself and his family. But this farmer left behind an extensive record of his times and the community in which he lived—though not in words. His photographs—over 400 of them—remain to tell the tale of W. R. Trivett's world.

Chapter II

Willie R. Trivett, Photographer

Farmer, carpenter, sheriff's deputy—W. R. Trivett was all of these, but his most significant lifework was as a professional photographer. From 1907 through the 1950s Trivett made images of the mountain people of rural Watauga and Avery counties, leaving behind over 400 photographs in his own collection. The story of Trivett's calling as a photographer is well documented—not only in pictures, but also in his surviving personal papers. His work was not especially unique, for he was one of many self-taught professional photographers who recorded the varied faces of Appalachia. Yet his story, along with the histories of other Appalachian "picturemen," illuminate the process by which the truest portraits of the Appalachian region were made.

W. R. Trivett and Haskell Trivett "making pictures" on Highway 67 at the Butler bridge, Tennessee, 31 July 1949.

The history of photography in America (especially its technical aspects) has been well plumbed by numerous historians of photography, art historians, museum curators, and many photographers themselves. Likewise, the careers of the American masters of photography of the first fifty years of the 20th century—Alfred Stieglitz, Edward Steichen, Walker Evans, and Dorothea Lange—have been examined and critiqued thoroughly. Yet the history of the legions of yeoman photographers who did not strive to create art with their cameras, but rather wrested a living out of taking pictures of children, sweethearts, weddings, funerals, and church revivals and singings, has been largely neglected.

W. R. Trivett and the other picturemen of Appalachia, however, form a unique class of photographers in the history of American photography. Between the late 1890s and the 1940s, these self-taught yet highly competent photographers worked on the fringe of the photographic world. Lacking the economic and educational resources of their counterparts in the towns and cities of Appalachia, the picturemen served as liaisons to rural patrons who could not afford either the time or the money to have their picture taken by a professional studio photographer. Thus W. R. Trivett and other Appalachian picturemen recorded images of people and places that otherwise might have remained invisible in the pages of history. This is the picturemen's greatest significance.

Before assessing W. R. Trivett's and other Appalachian picturemen's work, a brief sketch of the state of photography in America between 1830 and 1910 is helpful. In 1826 or 1827, a French country gentleman named Joseph Nicephore Niepce (1765–1833) produced the world's first photograph on a 6½ × 8 inch pewter plate. Some ten to twelve years later in 1839, Niepce's partner, Louis Jacques Mande Daguerre (1787–1851), perfected the photographic process which bears his name, making modern photography as it is known today practical. "Daguerreotypomania" quickly swept Europe and crossed the Atlantic to the United States where it flourished in New York, Philadelphia, and Boston.[1]

Improvements and advances in photographic technology (such as the collodion "wet-plate" method of making negatives on glass) during the 1850s made photographs increasingly available to more people in the nation. Particularly important in the burgeoning accessibility of photographs in the United States was the development in 1856 of "ferrotypes" (tintypes) by Hamilton L. Smith, a professor of chemistry at Kenyon College in Ohio. Tintypes were photographs produced on thin sheets of iron, ranging from the size of a coat button to 10 × 14 inches. They were cheap, novel, and became extremely popular all across the United States in the late 1850s.[2] Four tube cameras and the later multilens cameras of the 1860s allowed photographers to produce multiple tintype images on one plate, which could be cut apart with a pair of tin shears.[3] During the Civil War, many Americans were introduced to photography through tintypes produced by "camp-following photographers" who accompanied the armies, making portraits of the soldiers to be sent home to loved ones.[4]

Beginning in the late 1850s, and lasting nearly to the end of the 19th century, Americans' appetite for photographs continued to grow and was satiated through such "fads" as card stereographs and the carte de visite portraits so popular in the 1860s and 1870s. Indeed, these two phenomena of modern popular culture brought photographs to the American people en masse. Yet one person more than any other in the second half of the 19th century was responsible for making photography itself accessible to Americans, and indeed, the whole world. That person was George Eastman. He was to photography what Henry Ford was to the automobile; Eastman made photography accessible to the masses.[5]

Eastman's first step towards the democratization of photography came in 1878 with his successful development of reliable dry plate negatives.[6] This breakthrough in photographic technology freed photographers from the cumbersome, tedious, wet-plate system, which literally fettered the photographer to his or her darkroom. The images on wet-plate negatives would begin to fade ten minutes after they had been exposed, thus forcing the photographer to have immediate access to a darkroom.[7] Photographers were not long in adopting the quicker, easier, dry plates, and by 1880 Eastman's plates were being sold by E. & H. T. Anthony, the leading American photographic supply house of the day.[8] Indeed, it was dry plate negatives that launched Eastman's photographic empire; in the fall of 1880 he quit his job as a banker and became president of the George Eastman Photographic Company.

Dry plate glass negatives were a great improvement over wet plate glass negatives, but they remained less than perfect as the agent of worldwide, mass photography. Glass negatives were heavy and easily broken—much too fragile for the fumble-fingered public. They also necessitated that cameras be large and weighty, thus requiring the appendage of a tripod, which made cameras that much more unwieldy. Eastman, therefore, soon began working on developing a lighter, flexible film base on which to make negatives. After four years of labor, in 1884 he produced a film "consisting of a sensitized gelatin coated on paper, called stripping film."[9] The paper film earned this appellation because "after exposure and processing, the gelatin emulsion was soaked free of the paper and mounted on a plate of glass."[10] "Stripping film" and the intricate method of developing it was found wanting by Eastman and others, and so work continued on the development of a transparent and flexible film base. Celluloid film was the fruition of Eastman's and other chemists' labor, and in 1889 Eastman offered the film to the world's photographers. Lightweight, thin, durable, and highly flexible, celluloid film facilitated the birth of the modern, hand-held camera.

First marketed in 1883 as "detective cameras," the early hand-held cameras were made to look like books, luggage, paper parcels, and watches to enable the photographer to take candid shots of their subject(s) surreptitiously. (Some were even made to be concealed in hats and behind neckties.)[11] In 1888 Eastman introduced the most famous of all the detective cameras—the "Kodak"—so named by Eastman to be short and pronounceable in any language. Built 3¼ × 3¾ × 6½ inches, and looking like a finely crafted wooden shoebox, the Kodak (also called the "Brownie") contained a roll of paper stripping film long enough to make 100 two and one-half inch circular exposures. After the photographer took all 100 exposures, the Kodak was sent back to the Eastman factory where the negatives were transferred from the paper to glass, and prints were made. The camera was then reloaded with film and returned to the owner, all for $10, which was a lot of money at the time. As advertisements for the Kodak stated, "You press the button, We do the rest."[12] In 1889 the paper stripping film was replaced with transparent celluloid film, thus allowing those who wished to do so to develop their own Kodak exposures. The age of the "snapshot" was born.

Yet most professional photographers of the late 19th and early 20th century scorned celluloid film, "detective cameras," and "snapshots," associating the three with amateur photographic hobbyists. Hence glass plate negatives remained the first choice of professional photographers until 1912, when reliable, high quality celluloid flat film became commercially available.[13] It is notable that W. R. Trivett and most other picturemen used glass negatives well into the 1940s.

By the dawn of the 20th century, photography, thanks in large part to George Eastman, had been transformed from the high-minded pursuit of a relatively small cadre of professionals and elite amateurs to the popular pastime of millions of people all over the world. At Eastman's Kodak factory in Harrow, England, 8,000 negatives a day were routinely processed in 1899.[14] The schism between those who sought to elevate photography to the ethereal plane of Art and those who pursued it as a business or pastime became even greater. Or at least artistic photographers tried harder to distance themselves from their more plebeian sisters and brothers. As John Szarkowski states in *Photography Until Now,* "It was a common article of faith that art was hard and artists rare; if photography was easy and everyone a photographer, photography could hardly be taken seriously as an art."[15] Thus Alfred Stieglitz, Edward Steichen, and other photographers in America took the high road to acclaim and history, while those who produced the portraits of our grandparents and great-grandparents took another to obscurity. W. R. Trivett and the other picturemen of Appalachia (as well as other regions, such as the West and New England), fall into the latter group. They did not take snapshots, but they did not produce "high art." These are matters of interpretation, however, and will be discussed more in the next chapter.

Picturemen

The simplification of photographic technology (i.e., the dry-plate system) and mass production of cameras, negatives, and photographic paper in the late 19th century led many to take up photography all across the United States. Most contented themselves with taking snapshots with their cute little "Brownies." Others saw a way to make some money off the picture craze that was sweeping the nation at the dawn of the 20th century. Such was the infatuation for photographs that even the most isolated, backwoods farm families of Appalachia were willing to pay (whether in cash or in kind) to have their own pictures made. Indeed, today there can be found among many mountain families' photographs works which were produced by antecedents of the 20th century picturemen in the late 1800s. These photographs, large in size (often 16 × 20 inches or greater), look like a cross between a charcoal or chalk drawing and a photograph (see figures 2.1 and 2. 2). Little is known about how these curious photographs were made, and even less is known about the photographers. Perhaps inspired by these unknown photographers' work, W. R. Trivett and others, such as Thomas Rupert (T. R.) Phelps of southwestern Virginia, and Paul Buchanan of western North Carolina took up photography as another way to supplement their incomes.

From 1897 through 1939, T. R. Phelps practiced the trade of the pictureman in southwestern Virginia's Washington and Russell counties, approximately 50–60 miles northwest of W. R. Trivett's territory of work in Avery County, North Carolina. Phelps' work as a photographer supplemented his income as a grist mill operator and watch repairman. Every three weeks Phelps loaded his three-by-five camera and tripod, 12 glass plate negatives, and his watch repair tools into his buggy, and set off on a sojourn through Washington and Russell counties that culminated several

FIGURE 2.1. ORIGINAL PRINT 5" × 7"

*William Marion Milsaps and Janey Love Milsaps, ca. 1890s. "Charcoal photo-
graph"—antecedent of the 20th century picturemen's work.*

days later in Bristol, Virginia.[16] Along the way he stopped at farms to offer
the stud services of his stallion, repair watches, and take photographs.
Over the course of 42 years Phelps made nearly 2,000 photographs of
couples, children, families, family reunions, school and church groups,
lumber gangs, and harvesters at work.[17] Today the glass plate negatives of
his pictures are kept in the archives of Emory and Henry College, in Washington County, and have received the attention of various scholars.

In North Carolina, W. R. Trivett was not the only pictureman in
Watauga County in the first decades of the 20th century. A survey of the
county's newspaper, the *Watauga Democrat*, from the turn of the century
to 1920 shows that for a time itinerant photographers somewhat like Trivett enjoyed steady, viable business.

In the summer of 1907, an enterprising pictureman named A. J. Campbell ran his first ad in the August 15 edition of the *Watauga Democrat*
advertising his services as a photographer.[18] The ad stated that he would

FIGURE 2.2. ORIGINAL PRINT 5" × 7"

Frank Edmisten and Isadora Elrod Edmisten, ca. 1903. "Charcoal photograph."

be in the county seat, Boone, for three days during "the Association" (the Baptist Association's meeting of churches, perhaps) taking pictures in "the latest and up-to-date styles." He must have been well equipped, for he stated that "any size and style" of photograph could be accommodated—"from the size of a postage stamp to 8 × 10 inches." This suggests that he either had his own enlarger or multiple cameras. He closed his ad by guaranteeing his customer's satisfaction, and boldly left his name: "A. J. Cambell [sic], Artist."

Business for Campbell must have been good, for 11 years later he was still practicing his trade. His ad in the August 22, 1918, edition of the *Democrat* stated:

> To one and all wanting first class picture work done. Call at our tent, see samples, get prices, and consider the grade of work, and you will have work done if interested. Fathers, mothers, sisters, brothers, and sweethearts have your pictures made before departing for the war. If drugs and other photographic supplies keep advancing the picture

business will soon be a thing of the past. You will be compelled to go to the city studios for your work and pay enormous prices. Am at my gallery at Mable, N. C. [western Watauga County] each Saturday to Tuesday.

Call see me near Bethel church, Aug. 27 and 28th at the association. Will more than please you in prices and work. A. J. Campbell, Traveling artist.

Much can be learned about Campbell and the work of the itinerant pictureman from this ad. That Campbell ran ads in the newspaper suggest that his business was profitable and a major source of his income. Like farming, however, it was also seasonal—Campbell only ran ads in the summer months. Although he stated that he did have a gallery in Mable, it is very likely that he did most of his photography outdoors without a flash. Hence the summer months afforded the best conditions for outdoor photography.

It is evident that Campbell had a natural talent for advertising. In another ad he ran in the September 26, 1918, edition of the *Democrat*, he again stressed the transitory nature of the photographic business occasioned by the rationing of the First World War: "have some up-to-date photographic work done, as photographic supplies are limited and hard to secure. It seems that the photograph business will soon be a thing of the past in the mountains."

To those who were about to depart to Europe to fight to make the world safe for democracy, he admonished, "Boys have your pictures made before leaving for the camps, while you have the opportunity"—before getting fatally shot or otherwise horribly maimed on the fields of France.[19] Moreover, Campbell emphasized the pictureman's two primary selling points: the quality of the photographs—they were not snapshots—and low cost, compared to studio photographers. The most lucrative venues for the itinerant picturemen were large gatherings of people, such as church meetings, family reunions, and other civic occasions. It was no coincidence that in two out of his three ads, Campbell mentioned working at the meetings of the Baptist Church Association.

In the spring of 1919, another local photographer advertised his services in the *Democrat*, though not as creatively as Campbell. J. R. Hendrix of Boone ran this concise ad in the April 24 edition of the paper: "I am prepared to do first class photograph work of all kinds at reasonable prices. Copying and enlarging photographs a specialty." This was the last trace of the picturemen's trade found in the *Watauga Democrat*. By the 1930s the only advertisements for photographic work were placed by professional studio photographers.[20]

Avery County, North Carolina, in the first half of the 20th century was also the haunt of more than one pictureman. While W. R. Trivett photographed primarily in the northeastern section of the county from the early 1900s through the 1950s, Paul Buchanan of Mitchell County, North Carolina, worked in the southwestern portions of the county at approximately the same time. Interestingly, the two never met, nor knew of one another.[21] Buchanan's pictures caught the eye of photographer Ann Hawthorne in the 1980s, and she had a small collection of them published in 1993 in a book entitled *The Picture Man*. The book generated much interest in the nebulous careers of the itinerant picturemen of Appalachia, and through its brief biography of Buchanan shed some light on how these unique photographers worked.

From the 1920s through 1951, "Picture-Takin' Paul" (as Buchanan was known) roamed the mountain counties Mitchell, Avery, Yancey, and McDowell of western North Carolina, photographing on request those who wanted their image frozen in silver-bromide forever. When he started as a photographer, he traveled by foot. Later, he traded a mare's colt for a 1928 Chrysler. He photographed only part time, mostly on weekends, whenever he was not farming, sawmilling, or mining for mica.[22] The majority of his pictures were portraits taken outside (he did not use a flash), most of which he contact printed.[23] Buchanan offered enlargements and copies of old portraits by sending the photographs to New York to be processed there.[24] He kept no records of his photographic business, which, for a time, was quite profitable. Buchanan did remember charging 75 cents for four postcards; 5 × 7 prints were four for one dollar. Smaller pictures, made with his Kodak 116 or 120 camera, were cheaper; they could be purchased four for 50 cents.[25]

Paul Buchanan's main concern as a photographer was to make his pictures "good and plain."[26] They were to "look just like" the sitter, or else they would not sell. Such was the picturemen's pragmatic aesthetic. When asked why he did not take up photography as a full-time occupation, Buchanan responded, "Dogged if I knowed. A few days now and then I'd get tired of it. Somehow I always did dread finishing them up."[27] And by 1951 he found itinerant photography too time consuming and haphazard to be profitable any longer. He put his camera away for good after that, and the memory of his time as a pictureman was resurrected only by Ann Hawthorne's interest some 35 years later.

Even as Avery County's rural residents patronized the services of such picturemen as Paul Buchanan and W. R. Trivett, two professional studio photographers in the late 1920s and early 1930s also vied to capture and reproduce images of Avery County residents. Frank Carr (and his wife) and Clifton Laws ran a series of ads in the short-lived weekly newspaper the *Avery Advocate* between 1929 and 1930 which described the various merits of their respective studios.[28] While these ads do not touch on the work of W. R. Trivett or Paul Buchanan, they do reveal the nature of competition the picturemen faced.

The *Avery Advocate* was started by Frank A. Carr and his wife (who despite being the publisher was listed only as "Mrs. Frank A. Carr") in 1927.[29] Carr and his wife were both photographers, but in March 1928 they were ready to abandon photography in order to meet the demands of publishing Avery County's only newspaper. In the March 29 edition of the *Advocate* the Carrs ran the following ad:

PHOTOGRAPHERS ARE ALWAYS IN DEMAND

There is no photographer in Avery County and there should be for there is plenty of work for one to do.

There is a complete outfit available for both studio and outdoor work and it can be bought at a bargain by anyone who will operate it anywhere in the county.

Some bright young person can secure instruction in the photographic art in connection with the purchase of the equipment if desired. Men and women both make good in the business.

For particulars regarding this opportunity call at this office or address: Photographer

Care of *The Advocate*, Elk Park, N.C.

The Carrs were apparently not too successful in selling their photographic equipment; similar ads ran in the *Advocate* through April 1930.

Nevertheless, in January 1929 the Carrs were instrumental in establishing Clifton Laws as Avery County's premier studio photographer (indeed, perhaps Avery County's only studio photographer). Through 1929 Laws ran several ads in the *Advocate*, and his studio was on the second floor of the same building which housed the paper in Elk Park.[30] Christened "The Tip Top Studio," Laws' enterprise in the beginning enjoyed thriving business and praise for its work, according to Frank A. Carr.[31] The studio was well equipped and offered enlargements, took sitters at night by appointment, and also developed Kodak films.[32] Like the father of the "Kodak" himself, Laws encouraged everyone to take lots of snapshots. "Kodak time is here," Laws proclaimed in one ad, and continued:

> Nature is adding new beauty to our country every day now. Get the Kodak habit and preserve the many interesting scenes that come to you. Get the habit of sending your films to me and thus [be] sure of the best possible pictures your films can produce.[33]

In another ad that took up as much space in the paper as a full-length article, Laws magnanimously offered some professional advice to Avery County's amateur photographers:

> We are getting some poor films made so by the failure to get a background for the objects taken. Faces will be flat if taken with the sky or a bright field covered with sunshine for a background. If you want good, clear faces get a dark background of trees, bushes, mountains, or anything but a clear sky behind the object you are trying to take. Always bring your pictures to us when you can and if there is anything wrong we can tell you about it.[34]

Perhaps because of the worsening economic conditions caused by the Great Depression, in May 1930 the Carrs sold the *Avery Advocate* to Frank B. Schumann.[35] As their proprietorship of the *Advocate* ended, so too did their association with Clifton Laws and the Tip Top Studio. Free of the burdens of publishing, the Carrs in the summer of 1930 made their own venture as photographers for hire. "We Cover Dixie Like the Dew" was Frank A. Carr and his wife's confident closing line in the July 24 ad which inaugurated their business. They boasted 25 years of experience in photographing family reunions, college groups, conventions, church, and "other large gatherings."[36] Business, however, must have not been very good, for the Carrs ran no more ads after 1930. Likewise, Clifton Laws' studio must have succumbed to the Depression; his last ads came in late 1929.

The pages of both the *Watauga Democrat* and *Avery Advocate* show that photography was a part of modern American culture that was alive and well in the Appalachian region of western North Carolina during the first decades of the 20th century. And while picturemen such as W. R. Trivett and Paul Buchanan never had their names in the papers of their day (other than for their obituaries), A. J. Campbell and J. R. Hendrix did. Campbell and Hendrix perhaps represent a higher echelon of picturemen— ones who pursued their trade on more of a full-time basis. Yet the story of how these men got started in the photographic business remains a mystery.

In W. R. Trivett's case, however, his odyssey into the world of photography can be traced in the remnants of his surviving personal papers.

*   *   *

W. R. Trivett took up photography in the early 1900s first by developing what were called "sun pictures." As amateur photography swept the United States along with other infectious fads of the turn of the century (such as the bicycle), some photographic companies offered through the mail negatives of various scenes, people, and landmarks which could be developed out of doors with sunlight.[37] The process was simple: one need only put the print paper along with the negative in a holder, place the holder in the sunlight with the negative side up, and wait for the picture to develop within minutes.[38] The directions found among Trivett's papers pointed out that this took longer in cloudy weather. At any rate, the process captured Trivett's imagination, but merely developing "sun pictures" did not satisfy him for long. For he was not only interested in making pictures to pass the time or have fun. In photography Trivett found a hobby which, if taken seriously, could provide extra income. It was not as toilsome as hoeing tobacco or cutting timber, yet was at least as profitable as selling eggs, milk, and butter, as will be seen later. Moreover, photography was also a more creative and engaging form of work than any of the tasks mentioned above; it provided a respite from the repetitive dullness of farming.

In July 1907—the same summer A. J. Campbell placed his first ad in the *Watauga Democrat*—W. R. Trivett ordered through the mail what was probably his first camera from the Conley Camera Company.[39] The Conley Camera Company was based in Rochester—Rochester, Minnesota, not Rochester, New York (the home of George Eastman's photographic empire). While not a giant of Kodak proportions, the company nevertheless offered a plethora of cameras and photographic accessories. The company's Catalog No. 5, dating ca. 1911–1913, featured "box cameras" (a copy of the Kodak "Brownie" detective camera), pocket cameras, stereoscopic cameras, "specimen" cameras for pathological laboratory work, and view cameras.[40]

Trivett kept the 20-year guarantee for the camera, but the camera itself does not survive. (When Trivett stopped photographing because of ill health in the late 1950s, he sold most of his equipment to his wife's niece in Tennessee, who had set up her own studio.)[41] The guarantee does not give a description of the camera (it is referred to only as "Camera No. S82768"), and so it is difficult to know the exact camera Trivett ordered. Judging from the size of negatives Trivett used, however, the type of camera he used can be deduced fairly accurately. Over his 40-plus years as a photographer Trivett used four primary sizes of negatives: 4 × 3¼, 3¼ × 5½ (most often printed as postcards), 4 × 5, and 5 × 7. Given Trivett's subject matter—family, school, and church groups, and individual portraiture—the camera most suited to this type of work was (and still is) the view camera. The view camera in Trivett's day was the American equivalent of the British field camera, both of which were used primarily for outdoor photography of still scenes. Many photographers also used view cameras for formal groups and portraiture.[42] In the Conley Camera Company's Catalog No. 5, view cameras ranged in price from $26 to $72, which must have been quite an investment for Trivett. (This compared to the price of the ubiquitous box camera, which ranged in price from $3 to $5.)[43]

Over the course of the next two years (from July 1907 through May 1909), Trivett taught himself the art and science of photography. Various articles in his papers, such as letters from Montgomery Ward and other mail-order companies, provide a loose outline of his "education," and once again the U. S. Postal Service became the main agent of Trivett's learning. In August 1908 Trivett ordered a catalog of cameras and photographic supplies from Montgomery Ward & Company. That September he also ordered a pamphlet on developing from the John M. Smyth Company of Chicago. Another source Trivett added to his collection was the "A. B. C. Guide to Photography," ordered in May 1909 from Wehman Brothers of New York.[44] Other items found in Trivett's papers suggest that once he learned the fundamentals of the craft, he kept abreast of contemporary developments in the field, even if he did not adopt any of them. (Trivett never used a flash with his camera, nor did he utilize an enlarger.) Saved in his papers is a 1930 Eastman Professional Photographic Apparatus catalog, and the October 1934 issue of *The Southeastern Photo News*, a monthly publication of the Atlanta Photo Supply Company.[45]

By 1909 Trivett was ready to begin "making pictures" in earnest.[46] He had his own business cards made (see page 22) and also a stamp set which he used to stamp the back of his photos. The stamp read

> From Willie R. Trivett Photo Studio
> Whaley: N.C.[47]

After Trivett moved into the Harmons' Flat Springs home in 1926, he built his own "picture house" (darkroom) behind the house. A spartan

FIGURE 2.3

W. R. Trivette's Flat Springs home as it is today. (Photograph by Ralph Lentz II.)

little structure made of rough, sawmill lumber, measuring approximately 5' × 8', it still stands today looking for all the world like an outhouse with windows (see figures 2.3 and 2.4). His "studio," depending on where he was photographing, was as vast as the mountain landscape around him, or as confined as the facade of a woodshed, sawmill, or his own front porch. When he did not use nature as a backdrop for his sitters, Trivett often used one of two painted landscape backdrops. Other times he would use a quilt or rug, or a plain, neutral colored piece of canvas as a backdrop.

"Dear Sir, Am very well pleased with my picture I don't believ mine flatters me much though, as I told you."[48] Lilly Reese wrote these lines in a letter to W. R. Trivett in December 1909. She was pleased enough with her portrait that she enclosed in the letter 15 cents to pay Trivett for his work. So began Trivett's life as a professional photographer. Trivett was one of the few picturemen to save not only his negatives, but also the records of customers and sales of his prints as well. These records, sparse as they may be, show that in the decade between 1910 and 1920 Trivett enjoyed a profitable, steady business as a part-time professional photographer. Indeed, he had buyers for his pictures from as far away as Sunset, Washing-

FIGURE 2.4

The "Picture house." (Photograph by Ralph Lentz II.)

ton. In 1910, John Rominger, a friend who had grown up with Trivett, sent him a letter from Sunset ordering some photographs; he wrote, "send me them pictures and I will send you the mone at once."[49] Yet the majority of Trivett's patrons were neighbors—usually within walking distance. Trivett had a horse but never rode it; he apparently preferred to walk. He never owned a car, and it was not until his son was old enough to drive in the mid–1930s that Trivett ever utilized an automobile.[50] Most frequently people would come to his house to have their pictures taken or to drop off film to be developed.[51]

These two letters and a postcard requesting Trivett to come and take pictures at a family reunion in June 1910 are augmented by a tattered notebook dating ca. 1914–1915, in which are recorded some of the transactions of his photographic business that year (see appendix).[52] Recorded in faded pencil in Trivett's own rough scrawl are the names of several of his patrons, as well as the prices they paid for prints. According to Trivett's notebook, 20 people out of 32 had paid to have photographs made for them. (The other 12 people had not paid at the time Trivett recorded the information.)[53]

The total amount paid to Trivett was $7.94; the average cost per transaction was 40 cents, though he made some prints for as little as 5 cents.[54] His costs were low; in his notebook he wrote that he could develop six postcards for 20 cents, or roughly 3 cents per card.[55] Similarly, he developed 16 3¼ × 4¼ prints for 48 cents, or 3 cents per print. Thus, if he charged a minimum of 5 cents per print (as his notebook suggests), for developing 16 3¼ × 4¼ prints he would have made 80 cents—a profit of 32 cents or 40 percent.[56] Since Trivett did not specify the length of time in his notebook during which he made the sales of his photographs—was this the total amount of sales during one weekend, a month, or the whole summer?—it is difficult to determine exactly how profitable photography was for him. Some perspective can be gained, however, by examining some of Trivett's other means of income. For instance, in the same notebook, Trivett recorded that in the month of January 1915 he earned $3.17 by selling the produce of his chickens and cows.[57] And in comparison to 15 cents an hour for working in a sawmill (which is what Trivett earned in May 1907 when he worked at the W. M. Ritter Lumber Company's Pineola sawmill), "picture making" in the early 1900s appears to have been a fairly lucrative way to supplement one's income.[58]

The Photographs

Pablo Picasso once stated that "Painters paint; it is the only language they know"—the point being that the artist's work speaks best for itself. W. R. Trivett's photographs, then, converse mostly about people. The body of his work consisted of portraiture, whether it was of individuals, couples, children, or families. Of the 460 photographs found in Trivett's collection, 425 are portraits. This stands to reason; views of the mountain landscapes were plenteous and free to Trivett and most of his patrons, and few were willing to pay for pictures of houses and other still-lifes. The remaining photographs in the collection are of special occasions—weddings, baptisms, singings and revivals, and community gatherings, such as for WPA projects.

Trivett's wedding photographs recorded the solemnity, intimacy, and festive nature of various ceremonies in the mountains. Plate 3 shows a well dressed wedding party consisting of the bride and groom and their respective families from the 1910s or early 1920s. All are dressed in their finest—white shoes for the bride, groom, and best man, immaculate white dresses

PLATE 2. ORIGINAL W.R.T. PRINT 5" × 7"

A group of singers from the Piney Grove Church of Christ of the Poga community, Carter County, Tennessee, in 1930. The Poga community is approximately three miles west of Flat Springs. (From Carter County, Tennessee and Its People *by the* People of Carter County, Tennessee. *Elizabethton TN: Carter County History Book Committee, 1993, 147).*

for the bridesmaids, and ties for all the men. The preacher stands at the far right holding a Bible, signifying the holiness of the three way covenant made between man, woman, and God. More intimate are plates 4 and 5, which are portraits of two young newlyweds and a bride, respectively. In plate 6 Trivett captured the festive spirit of what appears to have been a mountain "chivaree"—"a noisy, boisterous wedding celebration, anticipated by many couples as proof of their belonging in a community, but occasionally having violent or tragic results."[59] Note that the man on the mule (possibly the groom) is holding a double-barreled derringer. It looks as if the mule, bedecked with flowers, is getting married too.

Other ecclesiastical events Trivett photographed included baptisms and revivals. Interestingly, funeral photographs are conspicuously absent among his negatives. The macabre practice of photographing the deceased

PLATE 3. ORIGINAL W.R.T. PRINT 5" × 7"

PLATE 4

PLATE 5.

Susie Hagaman Trivette (1898–1957), ca. 1918. Trivette attended Appalachian Training School (present day Appalachian State University) from 1918 to 1919. Afterwards she taught at the Kellersville, Rominger, and Ivy Ridge schools of western Watauga County until 1926.

had apparently passed by the time Trivett started taking pictures. Taken on September 28, 1941, plate 7 records the baptism of Monroe Ward in Beech Creek, Avery County.[60] Plate 8 appears to have been taken on Beech Creek during the 1940s as well, judging from the people's clothes. Trivett's photograph (plate 9) of the Flat Springs Baptist Church of Christ congregation during a revival ca. 1923 reveals some interesting details about the worshipers and their services.[61] Most notable are the two doors separated by the span of five men, which denotes the gender segregation

PLATE 6

Possibly a mountain chivaree.

of the church. One door (and hence one side of the church) was strictly for men, the other for women.

Occasionally Trivett photographed scenes of important local history. One such scene was the aftermath of the cataclysmic flood of July 15 and 16, 1916 (see plate 10). Taken on Saturday, July 16, on the banks of the Watauga River, the photograph gives a hint of the destruction wrought by the deluge. The *Biblical Recorder* was more explicit in its one sentence word portrait of the torrent:

> Thirty or more counties overswept; eighty or a hundred lives lost in the swollen waters; scores of railroad and county bridges swept away; hundreds of farms robbed of their crops ... many humble homes many lumber plants and cotton factories and grist mills, caught and tossed like toys in the raging torrents ... towns and villages isolated from each other and from the outside world; trains marooned for days at various points where the floods caught them and cut them off, and thousands of summer visitors marooned at our mountain resort; damage done which conservative experts place at from ten to fifteen million dollars; for once and for the first time, the strange cry for outside help to keep at bay the wolf of want coming from the most self-reliant and most independent of our people:—all go to show that fair Appalachia has been stricken to the heart by this monumental disaster.[62]

Watauga County itself suffered an estimated $200,000 in ruined crops, roads, and property, but no one lost his life. The editor of the *Watauga Democrat* reckoned that had it not been for "a kind Providence," damage from the flood in Watauga "might have been many times worse."[63]

PLATE 7. ORIGINAL W.R.T. PRINT 5" × 7"

Baptism of Monroe Ward on Beech Creek, 28 September 1941. Some of the emulsion has flaked off the negative, resulting in the distortion on the right side of the plate.

PLATE 8. ORIGINAL W.R.T. PRINT 5½" × 3¼"

Baptism on Beech Creek, North Carolina.

PLATE 9. ORIGINAL W.R.T. PRINT 5½" × 3¼"

Congregation of Flat Springs Baptist Church of Christ, ca. 1923–24. W. R. Trivett's wife and son are on the first row behind seated children, third and fourth from the left.

Trivett's camera was sometimes enlisted by local law enforcement agents to record the trophies of Prohibition—bootleggers. Plate 11 shows a man affecting the pose of a "G-man" with his pistol casually trained on his buddy who pretends to be a transgressor of the Volstead Act by holding a bottle of "home brew." Taken in 1925, plate 12 records deputy sheriff Lawrence Storie (third from right on the second row) and his posse's capture of a moonshine still in the Dark Ridge community of Avery County.[64] Storie began his career as a lawman at the age of 21, and stated that he had never had a shot fired at him in all his raids on stills.[65]

As evidenced by several articles in the *Avery Advocate*, the manufacture of illicit alcohol was vigorously prosecuted by local authorities throughout the 1920s and 1930s. "The nation may be voting wet and demanding hard liquor, but if any variety of that beverage is to be dispensed in Avery County it will bear the government stamp and seal, according to indications from the sheriff's office," proclaimed the *Advocate* in September 1933.[66]

Avery Sheriff W. H. Hughes was as true as his word; between January 1933 and May 1934 he and his deputies captured and destroyed 29 stills

PLATE 10. ORIGINAL W.R.T. PRINT 5" × 7"

Aftermath of the great flood of 1916, taken on the banks of the Watauga River, 16 July 1916.

PLATE 11. ORIGINAL W.R.T. PRINT 5½" × 3¼"

PLATE 12. ORIGINAL W.R.T. PRINT 5½" × 3¼"

Revenuers on Dark Ridge, 1925. Front row, left–right: Bill McCloud, Fred Moore, George Harmon, Pashley McCloud, Everett Cook. Back row: Jimmy Norris, Tillet Gryder, John Parlier, Grady Norris, Clyde Gryder, Ivey Storie, deputy sheriff Lawrence Storie, Cloyd Parlier, Marion Storie. (From Bessie Willis Hoyt's Come When the Timber Turns, *Banner Elk, NC: Puddingstone Press, 1983, 195).*

and approximately 5,059 gallons of illicit liquor in the county.[67] And Lawrence Storie's experiences notwithstanding, Sheriff Hughes and his deputies did on one occasion have to dodge hot lead from hostile moonshiners. On an evening raid on a still site between Plumtree and Ingalls in July 1933, Hughes, county jailer R. A. Shomaker, and deputy sheriff Adam Wiseman came under a hail of pistol and shotgun fire. None were successful in dodging all of the shots; Shomaker and Wiseman received wounds in the face and chest from the five shotgun blasts hurled at them, while the location of Hughes' wound(s) was not disclosed in the *Advocate*. Fortunately, no one was seriously injured in the brief melee.[68]

Sheriff Hughes became one of Avery County's "legendary" law enforcement officials, and the war on crime he waged in the early 1930s was duly appreciated (at least by the *Avery Advocate*). On the front page of the September 16, 1933, edition of the *Advocate*, the paper proudly reprinted a letter sent to Hughes from the Cranberry Lodge of Masons.

PLATE 13. ORIGINAL W.R.T. PRINT 5" × 7"

WPA workers on Flat Springs Road, late 1930s.

In it the officers and members of Cranberry Lodge No. 598, A. F. & A. M. stated:

> We feel that your efforts have been very beneficial to our community and county and have made it a better place in which to live and rear our children. Therefore, we ask you to accept our profound appreciation and our loyal support in the suppression of crime and the enforcement of the law.[69]

Other special occasions Trivett photographed were of a more positive civic nature; these were his photographs of WPA workers in the Flat Springs community in the latter half of the 1930s. Between October 1935 and February 1937, 19.8 miles of farm-to-market roads were constructed in Avery County by 300 WPA workers.[70] Work on Avery County roads included straightening dangerous curves, widening, surfacing with gravel or crushed stone, building culverts and bridges, and digging ditches for the proper drainage of road beds.[71] Plate 13 records a group of WPA workers (complete

PLATE 14. ORIGINAL W.R.T. PRINT 5" × 7"

with five young boys and two dogs) after having finished digging a ditch for
the road in front of Trivett's house in Flat Springs. Another photograph,
plate 14, documents another group of WPA workers at an unidentified
location in Avery County.

Children

Trivett's photographs of special events in the mountains are perhaps
of the most interest to historians. But of more interest to Trivett were his
portraits of children, for these were his best sellers; they comprise the majority of his photographs of individuals.[72] Some of them depict the stereotypical Appalachian urchin: barefoot, wearing patched overalls, shirt buttoned
up all the way to the collar, with a crushed, well worn cap on his head
(see plates 15 and 16). The image is quaint and romantic; the reality of
barefoot children in the mountains was often painful and full of deprivation. Ray Hicks, the nationally renowned teller of Jack Tales from Avery

County, who spent many of his boyhood summers barefoot in the 1920s and 30s, believed that "the romantic notion of happy barefoot boys must have come from city people, not from those who walked the rocky mountainsides."[73] Walking forest floors carpeted with chestnut burrs and sharp rocks, or steep, rough, gravel mountain roads did not make for pleasant recollections. Hicks recalled:

PLATE 15

> My feet would get callused and horny. But that didn't keep them from getting cut and bruised. See, the worst part of developing calluses is that they make stone bruises quicker than if the skin wasn't so tough...
>
> It bothered me so, going down yander to the gristmill and to the post office [Hicks lived on Beech Mountain]. It was an awful steep path. I'd go down the banks with corn or buckwheat on my back, going to the gristmill to get it ground. And off of a steep place, little rocks would roll under my feet and my toes would scoot back under ... tear the nails off and leave them hanging. Finally one toe slid back and got broke. It didn't grow back right, and so I had to start wearing a bigger shoe on that foot. Broke it at the joint and throwed it out of place. My toes is yet crooked.[74]

Other portraits Trivett produced were done using conventions still in

PLATE 16

use today in children's photography. The little lad in the wash basin (plate 18), and the two children dressed in white (plate 19) could, but for the antiquity of their dress, be mistaken for children born in the last decade of the 20th century anywhere in the United States. Similarly, plate 22 depicts two seemingly urbanite children of the late 1920s or early 30s. Only the split rail fence behind the car and the dirt road beneath betray the rural provenance of the scene.

Families, Groups, and Individuals

The rest of Trivett's photographs consist of families, groups, couples, and individuals. Many, such as plates 20, 21, and 1 (page 5), were taken at family reunions. They range from the sober, plates 26 and 69, to the less than sober (plate 57). (The latter will be discussed more in the following chapter.) Perhaps the most captivating of Trivett's photos are his portraits of individuals and couples. Each is as unique as the sitters. In his portraits of couples, most record the happy, carefree union of sweethearts (plates 27 and 28). Others, such as plate 24, show a more terse, less affectionate relationship. Trivett also often took photos of siblings together, predominately sisters; see plates 26, 29.

PLATE 17

Here and on the following pages are many more examples of Trivett's photographs of families, groups, and individuals. Captions will provide names when possible, but unfortunately few of the subjects could be identified.

PLATE 19

PLATE 18

PLATE 20. ORIGINAL W.R.T PRINT 5" × 3¾"

PLATE 21. ORIGINAL W.R.T. PRINT 5½" × 3¼"

The Green family, ca. 1947

PLATE 24.

Annie Potter and Roy Vines.

Opposite page, left: PLATE 22.
Opposite page, right: PLATE 23.

PLATE 26

Anna Mae Phillips, Genieva Phillips.

Opposite page: PLATE 25.

PLATE 29. ORIGINAL W.R.T. PRINT 5½" × 3¼"

Juanita Estep, Ruby Guy Estep.

PLATE 30. ORIGINAL W.R.T. PRINT 5½" × 3¼"

Opposite page, left: PLATE 27; *right:* PLATE 28.

PLATE 31

Identified members, standing (l–r): Cornelia Church, Mine Church, unidentified, unidentified; seated (l–r): Delpha Church, unidentified, ca. 1918.

Plate 32

Stacy Harmon

PLATE 33

PLATE 34

PLATE 35

PLATE 36. ORIGINAL W.R.T. PRINT 5½" × 3¼"

Farry Moody Palmer

Together with his couple, group, and family photographs, Trivett's individual portraits provide a rich mosaic of the Flat Springs community from the beginning of the 20th century through the 1950s. Of particular interest is Trivett's 1917 portrait of Edonton Mitchell (plate 37).[75] Mitchell was one of the patriarchs of the community; he was one of the 17 founding members of the Flat Springs Baptist Church, and when this picture was taken he was 112 years old.[76] He was born two years after Thomas Jefferson made the Louisiana Purchase, and died during the summer Woodrow Wilson spent abroad in Versailles, working to create a "league of nations." Trivett was also frequently called upon to photograph the local men of God in his community (plates 39 and 40). This included his friend Dwight Edmisten (1899–1973), pastor of Beech Valley Baptist Church (plate 40). Trivett had grown up with Dwight's older brother, Carl (1887–1961), and the two had had, in Carl Edmisten's words, "a good old time" prior to Edmisten's enlisting in the army in 1907.[77]

Dwight Edmisten was a man of the spirit; his brother was one who enjoyed more worldly pleasures. While stationed at Fort Sam Houston, Texas, in 1909, Carl Edmisten wrote happily to Trivett of the plenitude of bars near the fort: "I Drink Beer sometimes until I swell up Like a Frog."[78]

PLATE 39.

The Rev. Dayton Jones

Edmisten also enjoyed forays with the local women. In a letter to Trivett dated October 25, 1909, he recounted a prospective sortie with some of the ladies of Texas:

> They were Three Girls Passed here This [evening] in a Buggy and They Said "Hello Soldier Boy" and I Said "Hello Kandie Kid" and I Said "how is chances for a ride with you Girls" and They Said "Kid wait until Tomorrow and you can shur have a ride with us."

Opposite page, left: PLATE 37; *right:* PLATE 38.

PLATE 40

The Rev. Dwight Edmisten (1899–1973), ca. 1925.

*   *   *

For over 50 years W. R. Trivett in his spare time made pictures for
and of his neighbors. After the late 1940s he took few pictures to sell; the
widespread abundance of high quality hand cameras which enabled virtually everyone to produce sharp, plain pictures that "looked just like"
the subject, and the general rise in the nation's standard of living after the
Second World War put the picturemen nearly out of business. Just about
anyone who had an automobile in Flat Springs could afford to go to Boone,
or Mountain City, Tennessee, to have their picture taken in a studio, or
even a department store. Indeed, by the 1950s there was no need for a
traveling pictureman; everyone had become their own. So W. R. Trivett for
the most part put away his old view camera and took snapshots with a

PLATE 41

pocket camera just like everybody else (although he still developed them himself).[79] His glass plate negatives were packed away and stored in the picture house, and the loft of his woodshed. There they endured, to various degrees, the ravages of time: extreme temperatures, dust, dirt, rats, and curious step great-grandchildren who enjoyed breaking the strange looking pieces of glass.[80]

Towards the end of his life W. R. Trivett sold his camera and most of his other photographic equipment, but kept in his personal papers many articles connected with his beginnings as a pictureman. The images he left

Plate 42

behind in his negatives, though captionless, for the most part speak for themselves as to when and why they were taken. Yet they also raise many questions: We know what they are, but what do they mean—what do they tell us about the times, places, and people they keep crystallized forever? Can these quaint images be considered art? Of what value are these pictures, and indeed, the works of other picturemen in Appalachia, to historians? In sum, how should Trivett's photographs be interpreted? W. R. Trivett left no rustic treatise of his philosophy on photography, nor did he ever talk with anyone much about "picture making." He provides little insight into answering the aforementioned questions. The answers lie, however, in the careful contemplation and examination of his photographs.

Chapter III

The Photographs of W. R. Trivett and the Other Appalachia

Over 400 glass-plate negatives and perhaps some 100 original prints comprise W. R. Trivett's legacy as a self-taught professional photographer. For the most part, the images Trivett made of his neighbors, family, and friends in his spare time over a period of nearly 50 years have remained the private treasures of those who commissioned the photographs. Today prints of Trivett's and other Appalachian picturemen's negatives are being viewed and scrutinized by a much wider audience of scholars, historians, anthropologists, and other people interested in seeing Appalachia as it was seen through the eyes of the mountaineers themselves. And as the body of photographs made by Trivett in the first half of the 20th century are brought to light, they reveal a different portrait of the Appalachian region and its people. This is the Other Appalachia.

Yet "Appalachia"—the conception of the mountainous region of the southern United States as "a coherent region inhabited by an homogeneous population possessing a [unique], uniform culture"—is only a rather recent invention of the past 150 years.[1] What Trivett and other natives of the region thought about this conception of their homeland, which was largely foisted upon them by outsiders, will be taken up directly. First it is important to examine the invention of "Appalachia" and its inventors. For by the works of their minds—their words—and the works of their hands—their pictures—they formed the frame of reference by which all subsequent views of Appalachia have been perceived.

71

The invention and evolution of "Appalachia" has been chronicled in Henry D. Shapiro's *Appalachia on Our Mind: The Southern Mountains and Mountaineers in the American Consciousness 1870–1920* (1978), and more recently, Allen W. Batteau's *The Invention of Appalachia* (1990). Shapiro asserts that the idea of Appalachia as being fundamentally different and apart from mainstream American culture originated with American local color writers of the 1870s. These writers, both male and female, from North and South (but rarely from Appalachia itself), found and described the mountainous regions of east Tennessee, western North Carolina, West Virginia, and southwestern Virginia as "a strange land" populated by a "peculiar people."[2] To them the southern mountains were a land of "geological and botanical curiosities." The residents of the area mirrored the topographical strangeness in both their physical characteristics and their customs.[3]

Between 1870 and 1890, some 90 sketches and more than 125 short stories published the extraordinary "facts" of the "otherness" of the Appalachian region. It did not matter that most of the local color writers based their accounts on only certain aspects of mountain life, which they observed on vacations or on other short trips through the region; their writings were presented as typical scenes of everyday reality in the mountains.[4] The conception of the distinct "otherness" of Appalachia was reinforced by the writings of northern home missionaries who came to the mountains (and the rest of the South, as well) in the 1870s and 1880s to educate and reevangelize the war-torn legions of ex–Confederates and ex-slaves.[5]

The portrayals of Appalachia made by local color writers, Northern home missionaries, and progressive educators of the last quarter of the 19th century penetrated and made a home deep within the minds of the American public. But the images of Appalachia they presented were skewed. Shapiro points out that the local color writers were, because of the demands of their trade (i.e., to get published), compelled to report almost exclusively on the colorful, unusual, quaint, and picturesque in the southern mountains. Who would want to read about the mundane, average, bland reality of rural American life? For their part, the home missionaries through their writings had to convince their denominations and other philanthropic supporters of both the righteousness and dire necessity of their work among the poor, illiterate, and unchurched residents of Appalachia.

By the turn of the century, two basic images of the people of Appalachia had been created. One image was positive, the other negative, and both were frequently intertwined. At the heart of both conceptions was the "fact" of the region's isolation from mainstream, modern America. Essentially, a lack of urbanity—"the absence of industry, the absence of urban centers, the absence of the [social] institutions of community, the absence of a cash economy and a cash nexus as the basis of the social order"—defined the otherness of Appalachia.[6] Indeed, Allen W. Batteau has asserted that the conception of Appalachia was an invention of America's urban elite.[7]

Positively construed, the isolation of Appalachia had preserved the region from the manifold evils of the industrial revolution in America. In this "retarded frontier," as Chicago sociologist George E. Vincent referred to Appalachia at the turn of the century, the pure, uncomplicated ways of life of revolutionary America lived on.[8] Here modern, urban, hectic, confused 20th century Americans could look to the mountaineers—their "contemporary ancestors"—to rekindle the lost virtues of the pioneers. Isolation had also kept the mountaineers "racially pure," i.e., white, Anglo-Saxon, and Protestant. As such, the mountaineers were seen as an important repository of "traditional American values and patterns of culture," which during the late 19th and early 20th century was seemingly being threatened by the large influx of southern and eastern European Catholic immigrants pouring into the country.[9]

Conversely, the negative interpretation of Appalachia saw the region's isolation as the cause of a terrible physical, mental, and spiritual blight of the mountaineers. Lack of good roads and railroads had kept the region's economy retarded very near to the point of a frontier bartering system. The dearth of such social institutions as churches and schools had left the mountain people in a primitive, savage state.[10] Poverty marked the whole region. The romantic log cabin was described as a "hut"—a filthy, squalid, barren abode of ignorance, and often immorality. The mountains were a land of violence and criminality, of the blood feud and blockade whiskey. Here was the Appalachia that needed salvation in every sense of the word. Deliverance was needed for the degenerate, education for the illiterate, purpose for the indolent, sustenance and decent housing for the hungry.

At the dawn of the 20th century two contrasting images of the people of Appalachia had been grafted in the American consciousness. In the positive view the mountaineer was the descendant of the founding fathers' generation; a patriot, purposeful, industrious, self-sufficient; if uneducated, he/she was also unpretentious; imaginative, artful, tall, strong, proud, vigorous in old age, wise, trusting, friendly; the repository of the best of

America's heritage. In the negative view, mountaineers were seen as the children (probably illegitimate) of "exported paupers and convicts [indentured servants], and poor white trash"; they were anarchic, provincial, lazy, shiftless, poor, dirty; illiterate, ignorant, heathenish, immoral sexually and otherwise; violent, murderous, given to rage; thin, bent with age, wasted from years of little food and too much homemade whiskey; the anachronistic backwash of a savage frontier.[11]

Until recently, such has been the frame of reference for most people's perceptions of Appalachia. These divergent images of mountain people have been so pervasive as to pass for reality. In the heyday of the Appalachian picturemen of the 1930s, two books were published which continued to perpetuate what might best be called mythic Appalachia: *Cabins in the Laurel* and *Handicrafts of the Southern Highlands*. What made these works so compelling was not necessarily their words, for they said nothing new, but rather the photographs that augmented the texts. The combination of prose and artistic images was the key to the power of their vision of Appalachia. Yet while the written and photographic accounts of these two books were made at roughly the same time and among the same people as photographed by W. R. Trivett and the other Appalachian picturemen, the Appalachia they depicted was altogether different from that photographed by Trivett and his kind.

In the Grand Tradition—Cabins in the Laurel and Ulmann's Appalachia

In 1935 the University of North Carolina Press published *Cabins in the Laurel*, which quickly became regarded as a classic work on life in Appalachian America. Set in a section of the mountains of western North Carolina known as the Toe River Valley (encompassing Mitchell, Avery, and Yancey counties), the book was written by Muriel Earley Sheppard, a native of New York who moved to the area in 1928 when her husband, a mining engineer, was appointed field representative for the U.S. Feldspar Code Authority in the Southern District.[12] The Sheppards took up residence in the small town of Spruce Pine, in Mitchell County, where Muriel spent a good deal of her time visiting with neighbors, collecting folklore, and researching the history of the Toe River Valley.[13]

When the fruition of her cultural combing was published in 1935, it was augmented by 128 photographs taken by Chapel Hill studio photographer

Bayard Wootten. Wootten perhaps had closer personal ties to the Toe River Valley than Sheppard, for her cousin, Lucy Morgan, operated the Penland School of Handicrafts near Spruce Pine. Wootten first visited Penland in 1928, when she was asked to take pictures for a proposed catalog for the school.[14] In subsequent trips to the area, Wootten met Sheppard, who was using Penland as a research resource. This collaboration—Sheppard's prose and verse, and Wootten's images of mountains and mountaineers—produced one of the most arresting depictions of Appalachia ever made. It was a work of art, however, more of a poem than a narrative or documentary, that came to be taken for reality.[15]

Cabins in the Laurel might best be described as a look backwards. Sheppard concluded the book by asking, "Where does today begin in the hills, when yesterday has not yet left off?" Such was the frame of mind she apparently worked under while collecting material for the book. Much of her narrative was concerned with life in the mountains between the 1860s and 1900. In fact, many of the mountain residents she quoted were in their nineties, and gave firsthand accounts of the often chaotic and lawless prosecution of the Civil War in the Toe River Valley.[16]

When not recounting the golden years of the ante- and post-bellum mountains, Sheppard touched and elaborated upon nearly all the major tenets of Appalachian lore in her descriptions of contemporary life in Mitchell, Avery, and Yancey counties. In her account of the legendary woodsman and hunter of Mt. Mitchell, Big Tom Wilson, Sheppard presented the mountain man as one with nature. She even went so far as to allude to some of the hill people's bestiality when she described how one mountain family had raised a wolf pup, letting it nurse from a human mother's breast.[17]

Throughout the book Sheppard emphasized the mountain people's separateness from the rest of mainstream, modern America. To the people of the Toe River Valley, "Anyone who comes from somewhere outside the mountains is a 'furriner' ... whether he comes from Knoxville or New York or London."[18] She noted the local population's antipathy towards immigrant Italians, Germans, Russians, and the one Jew who were brought into the mountains in 1903 to build a railroad line from Spruce Pine to Spartanburg, South Carolina. The mountain people were especially hostile towards blacks, who were imported as a large part of the labor force in improving mountain highways in Mitchell and Avery counties in the 1920s. Sheppard stated that "The mountain people would almost rather not have the highway[s] than let in the Negroes."[19]

But if the people of the Toe River Valley were provincial, even racists, at least they were of pure Anglo-Saxon descent. And they had held on to their English heritage down to the 20th century. Sheppard here quoted at length from the English ballad collector Cecil Sharp's *English Folk Songs from the Southern Appalachians* (1917). On his trek through the Toe River Valley in 1915 Sharp found the mountain people's speech English, rather than American, and that they had "an easy unaffected bearing and the unself-conscious manners of the well bred."[20]

Unquestionably Sheppard's assessment of contemporary life in the mountains was romantic and nostalgic, and for the most part positive. If the hill man was lazy, it was because he had a higher value for time than the harried outlander. The suburban worker sold his or her time for money to buy possessions; the mountaineer sacrificed an abundance of things to spend precious free time.[21] And if many of the region's adults were illiterate, they saw to it that their children were not. Sheppard noted that in 1929–30 Mitchell County had educational buildings and equipment worth $263,975 with 3,395 white children and 8 blacks attending school.[22]

Sheppard's quaint vision of the Toe River Valley was reinforced by Bayard Wootten's accompanying photographs. Indeed, Jonathan Daniels in his review of the book in the March 30, 1935, issue of the *Saturday Review of Literature* wrote:

> Beside Mrs. Sheppard's interesting story the Bayard Wootten photographs splendidly serve to make reality of this Valley world. Unlike too many photographs, they do not serve to pull the reader's imagination down to a disappointing veracity from a stirring text.[23]

Plates 43 (page 77) and 44 (page 78) are representative of the particular reality Wootten's photographs convey. They are exemplary Appalachian icons—the old, bearded mountaineer, poor but happy. That the men were poor is evident by their worn, patched cloths, and their rough hewn surroundings; that they were happy is implied by the captions (which were taken from Sheppard's text) beneath the photos. The caption for Plate 43, which states, "If he feels like taking the day off, he will probably pick up a chair, tilt it against the sunny side of the house, and start enjoying the day," completely ignores the man's poverty.[24] Charles Alan Watkins also pointed out in his 1985 article "Merchandising the Mountaineer: Photography, the Great Depression, and *Cabins in the Laurel*" that the majority of portraits in the book depicted older men and women, rather than young and middle-aged adults.[25]

PLATE 43

Photograph by Bayard Wootten, from Cabins in the Laurel. *(North Carolina Collection, University of North Carolina Library at Chapel Hill. Used by permission.)*

PLATE 44

Photograph by Bayard Wootten, from Cabins in the Laurel. *(North Carolina Collection, University of North Carolina Library at Chapel Hill. Used by permission.)*

Missing from both Wootten's photographs and Sheppard's text were the middle and upper classes. Traces of modernity such as automobiles were few, and downplayed by both author and photographer. There are for example no pictures of the trains that came through Spruce Pine twice a day, and Sheppard stated that the trains "scarcely affected the character of life among the hill people."[26]

Thus *Cabins in the Laurel* perpetuated in both words and pictures the most persistent stereotypes of Appalachia. Even though most critics found *Cabins* "a thoroughly likable, instructive and entertaining book," Sheppard's neighbors in western North Carolina were outraged.[27] It should not be surprising that they objected to an outsider's portrayal of them as backward, illiterate, drunken hicks.[28] And because the book was viewed as being the product of "an extensive and intensive piece of research," Sheppard's account of life in the Toe River Valley was taken very seriously.[29]

The only other significant publication of photographs depicting life in the southern mountains during the 1930s came in Allen H. Eaton's *Handicrafts of the Southern Highlands*, published in 1937. It featured 58 photographs of mountain people and their various craftworks, such as coverlets, quilts, and handmade furniture. The pictures were taken in the mountains of Kentucky, Tennessee, North Carolina, and Georgia in the summers of 1933 and 1934 by New York City native Doris Ulmann. Although she was largely self-taught in the art of photography, she had studied for two years at the Clarence White School of Photography at Columbia University. Ulmann made portraits of many eminent luminaries during her career (such as Albert Einstein and Calvin Coolidge), but she is best known for her Appalachian photographs. In them, she managed to contrive a magnificent, albeit skewed, image of Appalachia and its residents.

John Jacob Niles, a ballad collector and singer, and Ulmann's traveling companion and sometime assistant on her photographic expeditions into the southern mountains, recalled that she was in search of certain types of subjects:

> [Of] all the people she photographed I believe the ones she loved most were the old mountaineers with white whiskers, the patriarchal types, and their ancient wives, though she also made many photos of young mountain men and women and their endless children.... She was willing to put up with any kind of weather, sticky heat or rain, or any kind of discomfort ... for the sake of getting to some remote spot where

some ancient sage and his woman-person might be found sitting in front of their cabin. And if the sage had a shock of white hair and a beard, her joy was complete.[30] [See Plate 56, page 99.]

Ulmann consciously sought those people who fit the Appalachian stereotype because she believed they were a disappearing species in modern, 20th century America.[31] Indeed, oftentimes the people she photographed did not at first meet her Appalachian aesthetic, as she once lamented, "They all want to go and dress up."[32] Yet, after photographing her subjects in the new, store bought clothes they wanted to have their picture taken in, Ulmann was usually successful in coaxing them into donning more traditional Appalachian garb. As Niles stated:

> [It was not hard] to get the women to put on their grannies' linsey-woolsey dresses, and then they would go into the attics or lean-to sheds and produce spinning wheels and portions of looms and some wool cards. They would gladly show us how their ancestors carried on, and then we would photograph them in these magnificent costumes.[33]

Plate 45 is a good example of Ulmann's vision of Appalachia. It shows what appears to be two daughters of the Revolutionary war era, barefoot, bonneted, and one can presume, illiterate. In his 1971 remembrance of Doris Ulmann, John Jacob Niles stated that one of the girls in the photograph later became an eminent doctor in Baltimore, and the other became a school teacher. Yet Ulmann's portrait of the two girls was staged to match urban America's conception of "Appalachia" in the 1930s. And a portrait of two stylishly dressed girls of the 1930s would not have been consonant with that conception.

Scholarly Views of Appalachia

Cabins in the Laurel and *Handicrafts of the Southern Highlands* were nonfiction works that did not purport to be objective, scholarly examinations of contemporary life in the Appalachian region. Nevertheless, they were taken as such by much of the reading public. During the 1930s there were two books which did offer scholarly analysis of the southern highlands and its population. *Culture in the South* (1935) and J. Russell Smith's *Men and Resources: A Study of North America and Its Place in World Geography* (1937) both contained studied, balanced views of the complex

PLATE 45. ORIGINAL PRINT 7⁵⁄₁₆" × 9¾"

Photograph by Doris Ulmann, from Handicrafts of the Southern Highlands. *(Used with special permission of Berea College and the Doris Ulmann Foundation.)*

realities of life in the mountains during the 1930s. Even so, these works also managed to affirm some of the most persistent stereotypes about Appalachia.

In 1935 the University of North Carolina Press published *Culture in the South*. Edited by W. T. Couch, a native of Virginia who was educated at the University of North Carolina, and who in 1932 became director of the UNC Press, the work was a compilation of 31 articles on various aspects of Southern history and culture. It was a massive volume, nearly 700 pages long, and was comprehensive in its appraisal of Southern culture, covering everything from the South's bittersweet Civil War legacy to southern magazines, black and white folk songs, and southern speech and humor.[34] Of particular interest is J. Wesley Hatcher's article "Appalachian America."

J. Wesley Hatcher was born in central Ohio in 1876, and was educated at Hiram College and Ohio State University, where he received his doctorate.[35] At the time he wrote the article, he was the head of the Department of Sociology at Berea College, Kentucky. He was also a minister in the Christian Church, and twice resigned his pastorate to work more intimately with the people of Appalachian Kentucky, Virginia, and West Virginia.[36]

Hatcher's assessment of the Appalachian region was unsentimental (though not without feeling), pragmatic, and a bit pessimistic in tone. He addressed the region's poverty first, which he attributed mainly to the poor use of existing suitable farmland, and the over-population of the rest of the marginal land in the region.[37] Next Hatcher discussed the region's valuable natural resources of timber, minerals, and labor—and their exploitation by outside interests.[38]

The most outstanding aspect of Hatcher's article was his acknowledgment of the complexity and diversity of the people who populated the region.[39] He maintained that there were at least three distinct classes within Appalachia. The first class tended to live in the fertile valleys of the creeks and rivers, where the farms and gardens were prosperous, and access to towns and cities was "relatively easy and many."[40] Members of the second class most often resided further up the valleys in higher, steeper, hills and mountains. Here the soil was thinner and poorer, and good roads less accessible. Hence agriculture yielded more modest returns, and living conditions were not as commodious as among the first class.[41] Finally, the third class lived in what Hatcher described as "the starvation points": the steepest mountains and darkest valleys; where the soil was terribly thin, and what little was there was nearly sterile. Access to the outside world was limited and only dearly gained. Isolation—both physical and psychical—had within this class rendered a strange land and a peculiar people. And as Hatcher stated, "It is the third group which has been held in the spotlight and is supposed by the American people to present the typical mountaineer."[42]

And it was on the third group—the "hillbilly" familiar to most Americans—that Hatcher devoted the majority of his time. Living in desperate poverty and isolation, these people had little or no hope, no confidence, no incentive to better themselves through work or education (both of which were virtually impossible to obtain), nor any respect for "the customs and values of outside society."[43] The word Hatcher used twice to describe the men and women of this benighted third class was "feral"—defined by *Webster* as "untamed; wild, savage ... deadly; fatal."[44]

It was here that the one room log house or "hut" could be found. They were dark (having at most one window), small, and filthy. There was no need to sweep the floor, for it was most commonly dirt. What little food could be found was served in a handleless skillet which served "as cooking utensil, hand basin, tub for family wash, vessel for toilet purposes."[45] There was no art in these homes—no quilts or coverlets, only the art of the poor—a bed made of poles, corn husks, or dry leaves from the forest, covered with rags.[46]

Life in the mountains, quipped one elderly woman of Avery County, was heaven for the men and dogs, hell for the women and mules.[47] In Hatcher's description, the third class mountaineer's physical and psychical degeneracy matched the squalor of their homes. His words give a terrible reality to the joke of an old woman:

> It is here that children are spawned and die like flies. Here is the source from which the feudist gets his mercenary. Here is where common law marriage prevails, illegitimacy is common, and incest is not infrequent. It is here that the woman is the convenience of the man. She is a beast of burden.... She drags the timber in from the forest, chops the wood with which the food is cooked and the family warmed. She cuts the timber from the hillside, grubs the stumps and undergrowth, and plants and cultivates and harvests the corn which keeps her and the man to whom she is a slave and their brood from absolute starvation. She is illiterate.... She is dirty and unkempt. She is ill-nourished and scrawny. She is stooped from the toil of the years since her early childhood, and wasted from much child bearing and from the excessive sex demands of an undisciplined, unoccupied and sensual man. Her clothing is scant

and vile and often in rags. She is aged and broken before she is thirty: to the casual observer she is fifty or more. She makes no complaint. She has known nothing better.[48]

It is perhaps marked with a preacher's hyperbole, but Hatcher's account was an accurate description of the wretchedness faced by the poorest of Appalachia's poor. He was careful, however, to point out that his outline of the third class was not a "photograph of 'the mountaineer,'" and that "No more is the Bowery a true picture of New York City than is the single-room, clayfloor, windowless log cabin a true picture of Appalachian America."[49]

Another scholarly view of Appalachia was published in 1937 in *Men and Resources: A Study of North America and Its Place in World Geography*. Written by J. Russell Smith, a professor of economic geography at Columbia University, the book was intended to serve as a geography textbook.[50] The book devoted three chapters to the Appalachian region, covering the Appalachian Ridge and Valley Region, the Appalachian Plateau and upper Ohio Valley, and the Blue Ridge and Carolina mountains. For the most part, the description of the Appalachian region as a whole, i.e., the great stretch of mountains and valleys extending from Pennsylvania to Alabama, is laden with statistics, maps, and relatively bland facts about the geography of the land, with a few observations about specific areas' social and economic development.

Concerning the central and southern part of the Appalachian plateau, particularly southern West Virginia and eastern Kentucky, however, the sterile tone of academic generalizations gives way to more colorful reporting. Of this area Smith stated that life for the people there had changed little since colonial times.[51] Many of the people were illiterate, but if they could read, Smith stated that "they read by the light of the hearth fire, as Abraham Lincoln read in his youth."[52] Yet Smith did note the lumber and mining industries' presence in the region, though he did not discuss how the railroads and other roads that came with them had affected (for good or ill) the people living there.

The section on the Blue Ridge and Carolina mountains continued in the same vein. In one paragraph Smith described the area as "an isolated land with moonshine whiskey and feuds for excitement, and where cornfields are set mid stones and stumps and the hill farms go to ruin by gullies."[53] At the same time, Smith did mention the burgeoning tourist industry in the mountains of western North Carolina, specifically citing Asheville as a "great center for tourists."[54]

*   *   *

A careful assessment of both Hatcher and Smith's scholarly views of
Appalachia shows that though they were more balanced and accurate than
Cabins in the Laurel, they too were tainted by some of the more pervasive stereotypes of the region. Concerning religion in the mountains, for
instance, Hatcher maintained that churches were only loosely organized,
with "no continuous, systematic activities"; records were not kept, and
money was not collected.[55] This certainly was not the case in W. R. Trivett's community, where the Flat Springs Baptist Church of Christ was an
active, well-organized institution which exercised (or at least tried to) some
means of social control over its members. Like many writers before and
after him, Hatcher asserted that "the mountain man is a thoroughgoing
individualist. No organization, political or religious, makes much appeal
to him."[56] Again, this did not bear true in the Flat Springs community.
Mertie Trivett's grandfather, W. M. Harmon, was a Mason, and a lodge
was held in the original Flat Springs Baptist church house for a number
of years.[57] Moreover, Hatcher (perhaps unconsciously) devoted the majority of his space and time to elucidating the sordid particularities of life
among the mountains' poorest class. This section is the most memorable
of the whole text.

Smith's *Men and Resources* is even more rife with Appalachian stereotypes. Indeed, the book has been called a "virtual compendium of racial
and sectional biases in vogue during the first quarter of" the 20th century.[58]
The comparison of mountain youths of the 1930s to the children of Abraham Lincoln's generation is a very good example of this. Still, Smith did
note that some parts of Appalachia were well integrated into modern,
industrial America. He cited the small city of Kingsport, Tennessee, with
its town charter that was conceived by experts in the New York Bureau
of Municipal Research, and its many industries, such as Kodak's photo-
chemical plant, Corning glassware, and textiles as representative of the
potential for sustained development in Appalachia.[59]

Despite their failings, Hatcher's "Appalachian America" and Smith's
Men and Resources offered a more realistic view of contemporary Appalachia than either *Cabins in the Laurel* or *Handicrafts of the Southern Highlands*. Yet in the 1930s, the vision of Appalachia that won out and lingered
in the majority of Americans' minds was that presented in the latter two
popular nonfiction books. Lacking captivating photographs and palatable
texts filled with colorful anecdotes about mountain people, the scholarly

works were doomed to low readership. *Men and Resources* was a text-book, after all. Thus, as is true today, Americans' conceptions of Appalachia were largely formed and dictated by urban, popular culture.

Cabins in the Laurel and *Handicrafts of the Southern Highlands* are examples of how most outsiders viewed Appalachia and its residents in the 1930s. But as Allen W. Batteau has stated, "'Appalachia' is a frame of reference, not a fact."[60] The photographs of W. R. Trivett show that he and the mountain people who commissioned their own portraits did not share the same frame of reference when thinking of themselves as Muriel Early Sheppard, Bayard Wootten, or Doris Ulmann. Next, images of "the other Appalachia"—mountain people as they viewed themselves—will be seen and considered.

Interpreting the Picturemen's Work

Before examining this other Appalachia, it is first necessary to address some key questions concerning W. R. Trivett's photographs. How should they be interpreted? Are they works of art or documents? How and why were they made?

The question "What is Art?" is nearly as confounding as Pilate's question "What is truth?" While it is acknowledged that there are very few master artists, everyone (at least in his/her own eyes) is a critic, and thus everyone's definition of art is different. Since its invention in 1839 there has been a debate as to whether photography is truly a fine art. In America the work of Alfred Stieglitz, Edward Steichen, Walker Evans, Dorothea Lange, Ansel Adams, and others have helped to confirm photography's claim as a legitimate art. Whatever today's critics think, there is evidence which suggests that some of the Appalachian picturemen considered themselves artists.[61] A. J. Campbell, the itinerant photographer who ran ads in the *Watauga Democrat* from the early 1900s through the teens, often added the appellation of "Traveling artist" to his name in his advertisements. Still, the picturemen did not produce high art. Most did not have the resources—i.e., time, training, and equipment—to do so. But "high art" was never their aim. Thus the work of the itinerant picturemen of Appalachia is perhaps best interpreted as a type of folk art. Jerald Maddox, past curator of photography at the Library of Congress, defined this type of photography as

PLATE 46

not primarily concerned with either technology or aesthetics, although
it will make use of both as seems necessary. Instead, the primary interest of this type of photography is simply the making of photographic
images as a visual record, as a means of preserving certain events or
objects, [or people] without any further complications or involve-
ments.[62]

Yet, as Charles A. Watkins asserts in his 1997 article "Why Have
There Been No Great Appalachian Photographers?" quibbling over the picturemen's aesthetics is not as important as interpreting the content of their
unique images.[63]

Can the photographs of W. R. Trivett be considered documentary? It
depends on the definition of "documentary." Without a doubt the bench-
mark for judging documentary photography in 20th century America is
the huge corpus of photographs taken by the Farm Security Administration's historical division under the aegis of Roy E. Stryker from 1935 to
1943.

PLATE 47

The impetus behind the FSA photographs was to justify pictorially to the American public the activities of the Resettlement Administration, later the Farm Security Administration. Created by President Franklin Roosevelt's Executive Order 7027 on April 30, 1935, the Resettlement Administration was charged with providing much needed relief for the nation's beleaguered farmers, who had been suffering the effects of severe economic depression since 1920. This entailed a number of programs, such as low interest loans to poor farmers, soil rebuilding and conservation, and resettlement of destitute farmers.[64] Resettlement of farmers—which sometimes involved the setting up of government sponsored communal farms and rural communities—was extremely controversial, and sent critics of the Roosevelt administration to howling charges of red Communism.[65] Roy Stryker and the FSA photographers' objective, then, was to first show the widespread deprivation of the nation's farmers to the public, and later, to show the success of the Resettlement Administration's programs. In short, the documentary photographs of the FSA were propaganda.

But how can documents be propaganda? Propaganda, after all, consists of lies, while documents are truth. At least this is the conception in many American's minds; since the onset of the Second World War Americans have been taught that propaganda is strictly the purview of fascists,

PLATE 48

Communists, and other depraved groups perceived as threatening to democracy and freedom. Yet propaganda, as defined by *Webster*, is merely "any systematic, widespread dissemination or promotion of particular ideas, doctrines, practices, etc. to further one's own cause or to damage an opposing one." The term "documentary," as William Stott convincingly shows in *Documentary Expression and Thirties America* (1973), has many meanings.

Documentary has been defined as "presenting facts objectively and without editorializing and inserting fictional matter, as in a book, newspaper account or film."[66] Stott elaborates further that there are two tendencies within the documentary genre—the first, to inform the intellect, and

PLATE 49

the second, to inform the emotions.[67] In social documentary, facts are reported to enlighten both the intellect and emotions, with the goal of encouraging social improvement. In its mildest form it is "public education"; at the other extreme it is what Stott refers to as "that maligned thing, propaganda."[68] Lewis Hine, whose photographs of the terrible realities of child labor in textile factories and coal mines in the early 1900s helped to pass the first legislation protecting child laborers, perhaps defined the social documentary attitude best when he said, "I wanted to show the things that had to be corrected. I wanted to show the things that had to be appreciated."[69] The photographs of the FSA were social documentary in form.

PLATE 50

They were a presentation of actual facts in a way that made them especially compelling to people at the time, all in the effort of bringing about social change.[70]

W. R. Trivett's photographs, then, were documentary only in the sense that they documented what was before his camera. They were not taken to record any great social ill, such as rural poverty, nor to preserve the fleeting remnants of preindustrial American material culture, as was the purpose of Doris Ulmann's photographs in *Handicrafts of the Southern Highlands*.[71] Neither was chronicling everyday life the main objective of the picturemen. As David Moltke-Hansen stated in his 1994 article "Seeing the Highlands, 1900–1939: Southwestern Virginia Through the Lens of T. R. Phelps," the picturemen were "commissioned by friends and neighbors to record the ritual high points of their lives—christenings, marriages, family and church picnics—as well as loved ones in their Sunday best."[72]

The process by which Trivett made his patrons' portraits bears examining as well. While masters of photography such as Dorothea Lange, Arthur

Rothstein, and even Walker Evans (though he never admitted it), routinely took series of pictures of their subjects and then culled the best print (or prints) for presentation, W. R. Trivett generally made only one or two negatives of his subjects.[73] With Trivett this was probably more of an economic imperative rather than any aesthetic tenet. Plates were not that expensive, but to make a profit on his pictures Trivett had to keep his costs low and his prints affordable; therefore multiple exposures of the same subject to obtain a perfect image was not economically expedient. The picturemen had to get their pictures right the first time. And for the most part, they were remarkably adept at doing so.[74]

W. R. Trivett's working relationship with his patrons was largely dictated by the equipment he used to photograph them with. The view camera he used was a ponderous contraption. James Agee described Walker Evans' 8 × 10 view camera in *Let Us Now Praise Famous Men* as a "terrible structure of [a] tripod crested by [the] black square heavy head, dangerous as that of a hunchback, of the camera."[75] Use of a view camera required the photographer to make numerous preparations before exposing the film. First the photographer had to don the black cloak attached to the camera—used to block out light so he/she could see the scene before him/her on the tiny viewing screen—and then begin to compose and focus the camera. Next, he/she had to judge the available lighting of the scene, and most importantly, estimate the proper exposure time. Finally, the photographer had to prepare the sitters by asking them to stay still for the duration of the exposure.[76]

Thus the view camera necessitated a kind of covenant between the photographer and those being photographed. Sitters were obliged to be still for the period of exposure; the photographer was obligated not to photograph them unawares.[77] Trivett's customers, therefore, played a central role in creating the images produced by his camera. They chose their own dress and demeanor, if not their own poses. (Trivett often posed his sitters, or suggested poses for them.)[78] W. R. Trivett took no candid photographs.

In his 1901 treatise *Photography as a Fine Art* Charles H. Caffin defined two distinct types of photography—"the utilitarian and the aesthetic."[79] The former's main objective was a record of facts; the latter's was the expression of beauty. America's master photographers were the high priests of the religion of aesthetics. Walker Evans, Dorothea Lange, and others took photographs which, as Caffin stated, "[recorded] facts, but not as facts ... [the] object being not to get at facts, but to express the

PLATE 51. ORIGINAL W.R.T. PRINT 5½" × 3¼"
Lowella Guy, Juanita Ward Guy, Faye Guy Phillips, ca. 1943.

emotions with which the facts affected [the photographer]."[80] W. R. Trivett and the other picturemen, however, were primarily concerned with communicating what their sitters wanted to see. And this perhaps is the seminal factor in interpreting the images of the picturemen: their photographs were reflections of how the sitters saw themselves.

Pictures of the Other Appalachia

Manifested in such works as *Cabins in the Laurel* and *Handicrafts of the Southern Highlands*, the popular conception of Appalachia has for the most part been manufactured by outsiders to the region. Muriel Early Sheppard, Doris Ulmann, and Bayard Wootten were all natives of other regions of the nation. They all shared a distinct vision of a very particular Appalachia, which they, like legions before them, proffered as the whole reality of the region. To them, Appalachia was a region comprised mostly of senior citizens. It had a monolithic culture that was primarily folk and anachronistic. The majority of its residents were poor, lower class, and

PLATE 52

lacking in education. Many were illiterate. Most of all, it was a region and people cut off from mainstream, modern America. The people were not in touch with current fashions, modern modes of transportation, radios, motion pictures, or telephones; they knew little of the news of the world beyond the hollows and coves of their mountains.

This particular Appalachia was also emphasized by scholars during the 1930s, as seen in the writings of J. Wesley Hatcher and J. Russell Smith. Yet the photographs of W. R. Trivett reveal a different view of Appalachia.

Before his camera stood people who did not look or think of themselves as being separate or different from other Americans of their day.

The collective image Trivett's photographs produce of Appalachia becomes even more telling when viewed in the light of other historical information about the area in which he worked. If much less enjoyable reading than *Cabins in the Laurel* or *Handicrafts of the Southern Highlands*, census records of Avery and Watauga counties from 1920 and 1930 provide very interesting information about the people in W. R. Trivett's photographs.[81]

In 1920, Beech Mountain township was home to Trivett and 913 other people. The community was made up of 171 homes, of which 130, or 76 percent, were owned outright.[82] This would seem to indicate a relative high standard of living. Most of the community's residents were farmers.[83] Yet the 1920 census records show that among the 28 percent of people who did not farm to make a living, there was a diverse range of other occupations. There were for instance 11 people who worked at a nearby rubber factory. A number of others were lumber-mill laborers, including a 33-year-old woman.[84] There were three retail merchants, two in dry goods and one in groceries. Six people were professional scholars (that is, teachers), and there were two ministers in the community as well.[85] The presence of different occupations practiced in the Beech Mountain township suggest the existence of different social classes within the community.

Perhaps the most significant information provided by the 1920 census when comparing stereotypical Appalachia to the reality of the Beech Mountain community is that on the rate of illiteracy. Seventy-seven people, or 8 percent of the population of Beech Mountain township, were unable to read or write.[86] Illiteracy was spread fairly evenly between the two genders, with 32 males (42 percent) and 45 females (58 percent) being listed as completely illiterate.[87] Roughly 31 percent of those listed as illiterates were 50 or older.[88] Born in the decade immediately following the Civil War, this age group had fewer opportunities to acquire an education, due to the extreme lack of revenue available in western North Carolina to fund public schools in the desperate years of Reconstruction.[89] The rate of illiteracy for the whole of Avery County in 1930 was only slightly higher at 10.6 percent; that for Watauga County in 1930 was 7.8 percent.[90]

Clearly, these statistics produce a different image of Appalachia—or at least that part of Appalachia comprised of Avery and Watauga counties. Does it seem credible that 76 percent of lower class, poverty stricken people in the township of Beech Mountain in 1920 could own their own homes?

PLATE 53

It depends. If their homes were shacks or "huts" built just before, during, or after the Civil War, then the answer might be "yes." Statistics, after all, can be misleading. (Mark Twain put them one notch below "damn lies" for reliability.) Here is where the photographs of W. R. Trivett and other picturemen can be very helpful to the otherwise blind historian. For they reveal in clear, graphic detail at least a part of the material substance of the sitter's lives.

Among W. R. Trivett's body of work are a few photographs which can be considered as "typically Appalachian." (See plates 46, 47 [pages 87–88], plates 54, 55 [pages 97–98] and plate 12 [page 46].) Pictures of the aged, backwoods hunters, a busted moonshine still, and a wagon and team of mules in mountain mud: these images depict the stock icons of stereotypical Appalachia. It is critical to keep in mind, however, that these photographs were not taken for the purpose of exposing or exploiting mountain stereo-types. They were not destined for publication in any book or magazine, but

PLATE 54. ORIGINAL W.R.T. PRINT 5½" × 3¼"

rather for family albums. Consider the ancient couple's portrait in plate 54. It was likely commissioned by the sitters' family, perhaps by either their children or grandchildren. The exact date of the picture is hard to ascertain; the sitters' clothing looks as if it were tailored sometime in the postbellum years of the 19th century. It is probable that the photograph was made between 1900 and 1930. At any rate, it is apparent that the couple lived most of their lives in the 19th century, and it stands to reason that in their old age they would not abandon the fashions they had been accustomed to from the days of their youth. The two cross-cut saws in the background perhaps serve as indicators of a lifetime of hard, honest labor. Notable too is how the husband has chosen (or W. R. Trivett suggested) to show his large, weathered hands by folding his arms across his chest. In all it is a solemn, dignified portrait. No doubt a copy of the print became a treasure for the couple's family, including their later descendants.

Plate 55 shows three proud bear hunters and the reward of their hunt. In this picture, taken in the 1940s, the hunters are showing off their bear dogs.[91] At first glance this photograph, and plates 12 and 46, look unquestionably like representations of the mountaineers written about by John Fox, Jr., Muriel Earley Sheppard, and others. But upon closer examination, it becomes apparent that the pictures are lacking in some of the fundamental

PLATE 55. ORIGINAL W.R.T. PRINT 5½" × 3¼"

Dudley Trivett, Leonard Story, and Willie Harmon

iconography of conventional Appalachia. Missing, for instance, are long beards for the men. Plate 12 shows deputy sheriff Lawrence Storie well dressed and clean shaven for his and his posse's portrait with the dismantled still from Dark Ridge. Moreover, as Charles Watkins has pointed out, this photograph shows a law abiding community that did not tolerate the drunkenness and lawlessness associated with blockade whiskey—hence the broken-down still.

But perhaps the most important thing that can be said about these types of pictures found in Trivett's and other picturemen's collections is that they do not in and of themselves portray backwards, poor, illiterate mountain people. They can be interpreted that way, but the people in the photographs most certainly did not think of themselves in this manner. How many people are willing to pose for a picture that they know beforehand will depict them unflatteringly—as stupid, poor, dirty? Such was the reason for the outrage of Muriel Sheppard's neighbors upon first reading *Cabins in the Laurel*. They were not pleased with how their community had been interpreted. As John Ehle states in the foreword to the 1991 edition:

> The first mountain person to read a copy of this book must have real-
> ized it was not a description by a progressive writer of a progressive

PLATE 56. ORIGINAL PRINT 7⁵/₁₆" × 9³/₄"

Photograph by Doris Ulmann, from Handicrafts of the Southern Highlands. *(Used with special permission of Berea College and Doris Ulmann Foundation.)*

Plate 57

Identified members, left to right: Troy Guy, Ruben Potter.

people ... Hurt. The people had their feelings hurt; their pride, always close to the surface, was cruelly mashed. They had hoped for better....[92]

Other of Trivett's photographs reflect the sitters' sense of humor and knowledge of mountain stereotypes.[93] Examples of these lighthearted images are found also in the works of other Appalachian picturemen such as Paul Buchanan and T. R. Phelps. David Moltke-Hansen stated in his analysis of the work of T. R. Phelps that Phelps and his patrons often "seem to have amused themselves by staging scenes that poked fun at the stereotypes held by city tourist, the ethnographer, and the social reformer or Puritan."[94] Plate 57 is a splendid example from W. R. Trivett's collection of this type of picture. This photograph, taken in the late 1920s or early 1930s, shows four supposedly inebriated young mountain men.[95] Troy Guy, first person on the left, raises his right hand as if about to make a proclamation against the evils of drinking. Ruben Potter, the young man in the middle holding the bottle, looks like he has already had a snort. Plate 58 shows two young men affecting the pose of feuding hillbillies. One holds a pocketknife to his pal's throat while the other points

PLATE 58

what looks like a small semi-automatic pistol at his knife-toting friend.

The previous seven photographs just discussed constitute what can be considered a view of "traditional" Appalachia. Yet the overwhelming majority of the rest of Trivett's photos—some 452 images—present another Appalachia that has been little noticed. This Appalachia was populated not with a strange, separate people, but rather with very average looking Americans from the first half of the 20th century. A few were poor or wealthy; most were middle class. Both young and old—and those in between—were present in Trivett's community, as is evidenced by his many portraits. Just like the rest of rural America, most of the people made their living by farming. It is this image of Appalachia found in the body of W. R. Trivett's photographs which makes his and the work of other picturemen so valuable. For they show (as much as any one-dimensional record of the past can), that the majority of people who happened to live in the mountainous region of the southern United States during the first half of the 20th century had more in common with contemporary Americans than they did with their pioneer ancestors.

J. Wesley Hatcher in 1935 described the mountain man as a "thoroughgoing individualist"—a person divorced from organized religion, political party, and allegiance to any entity not within the shadow of familiar mountains. A number of W. R. Trivett's photographs refute this description. This is not to say that some mountain people were not this way, but rather that many considered themselves so much a part of the nation—that is as citizens of the United States first, and as southerners or mountaineers second—that they were willing to put their lives in mortal danger for national causes. Trivett's photographs of service men and women of the Beech Mountain community from the decades of the First and Second World Wars graphically illustrate this.

Plate 59 shows a veteran and members of his family. The veteran, seated on the right, wears a military cross of some sort on his left lapel, and on his right hangs what appears to be a purple heart. Plates 60 through 62 are portraits of servicemen from the teens through the 1940s. They had many other comrades in arms throughout Avery County. During the Great War, 421 Avery County men (11 of whom were black) served in the army. One woman, Ms. Hazel M. Patton, served as a nurse. Forty of the veterans bore the marks of their service in the form of wounds; four succumbed to disease, and two were mortally wounded.[96] In the Second World War, 1,469 Avery County residents served; 43 gave their lives.[97] Neighboring Watauga County sent 290 men overseas to make the world safe for democracy in 1917–1918, 21 of whom were killed. During the Second World War, 2,200 Wataugans served in the armed services. Sixty-three did not make it back alive.[98]

Of course, the families of the veterans were intimately connected with national affairs during the times of warfare. Plate 63, a portrait of Lowella

PLATE 59. ORIGINAL W.R.T. PRINT 5½" × 3¼"

PLATE 60

PLATE 63

Lowella Guy Ward

Guy Ward and her baby, shows that mountain civilians were just as affected by the total war of 1942–45 as other Americans. Perhaps to memorialize her husband or another member of her family who was overseas, she wears a "U. S." insignia and a "V" pin for victory on the collars of her blouse. Yet it was not just in the patriotic fervor of war time that the residents of Avery and Watauga counties felt part of the nation. Taken probably in the late teens or early twenties, plate 64 shows a small group of school children

Opposite, left: PLATE 61. ORIGINAL W.R.T. PRINT 5½" × 3¼".
Opposite, right: PLATE 62. ORIGINAL W.R.T. PRINT 5½" × 3¼".

PLATE 64

proudly holding the "Stars and Stripes." No doubt they were taught the pledge of allegiance just like children elsewhere throughout the United States. These were Appalachian people who were in and of America.[99]

Indeed, W. R. Trivett's photographs abound with signs of modern American culture in the midst of the mountains of Avery and Watauga counties in the first half of the 20th century. The automobile—perhaps the most potent symbol of modern America during the 1920s and 1930s—shows up not infrequently in Trivett's photos. (See plates 11, 65–68.) Plate 65 shows five automobiles that made it up to Beech Mountain for a special gathering sometime in the 1920s. When available, Trivett often used automobiles as a compositional device; they served as excellent props

PLATE 65. ORIGINAL W.R.T. PRINT 5½" × 3¼"

Cars on Beech Mountain

PLATE 66. ORIGINAL W.R.T. PRINT 5½" × 3¼"

PLATE 67

for people to pose on (see plates 66 and 67). It is interesting to note the people's poses with their automobiles, for they give a clue as to how supposedly
secluded, shut-off mountaineers thought of the newfangled means of transportation. In plates 11 and 68 the people lean against their car in a casual,
nonchalant manner, suggesting both their pride in ownership and their com-
fortable, cosmopolitan familiarity and acceptance of modern technology.

Yet the most salient evidence of Trivett's patrons' contact with and
acceptance of modern, popular American culture is in the clothes they chose

PLATE 68

to wear for their portraits. There is a great variety in the types of clothes worn by Trivett's sitters; they reflect the variety of people from different socioeconomic groups whom he photographed. There are pictures of men in the farmer's business suit (overalls) with ties on (see plate 70); other men appear in dapper three-piece suits—see plate 40 of Dwight Edmisten, and the five young men photographed on the steps of Watauga Academy in Butler, Tennessee (plate 69).[100] The ladies, almost without exception, are dressed in the latest fashions—à la Montgomery Ward. Take for instance plate 71, an early 1920s portrait of Mertie Trivett, her sister Hessie Weaver, and their sister-in-law Vergie Trivett. All three are decked out in hats and coats which came "direct from New York's fashion district" (according to

PLATE 71

the 1922 Montgomery Ward catalog; see Fig. 3.1).[101] "Wear an approved, authoritative New York style and make a worthwhile saving of dollars besides"—it was advice that Mertie Trivett and millions of other rural customers of Montgomery Ward's catalogs took in the 1920s and 1930s.[102] Indeed, many of the people photographed by Trivett would serve well for

Opposite page, left: PLATE 69. ORIGINAL W.R.T. PRINT 4" × 4¾". *Scholars at Watauga Academy, Butler, Tennessee ca. 1920.*
Opposite page, right: PLATE 70. ORIGINAL W.R.T. PRINT 4" × 3¼".

10 C 52
Velour Coating
Full Lined
$7.98

10 C 62
Velour Coating
$8.98

10 C 58
All Wool Coating
Full Lined
$17.98

10 C 66
All Wool Velour
Full Silk Lined
$29.50

10 C 70
All Wool
Polo Coat
$15.98

10 C 52 Attractive, and warm will be this Coat of Velour Coating about three-fourths wool. Brown Coney fur collar. Full Sateen lined. WOMEN'S SIZES: 34 to 46 bust.
LENGTH: about 47 inches. State actual bust measure
10 C 52—Medium Brown. PRICE,
10 C 54—Navy Blue. Postage,
10 C 56—Black. 16c extra $7.98

10 C 66 Extremely smart All Wool Velour Coat, full Silk lined. Collar and cuffs of Beaverette (sheared Coney fur). Richly embroidered on sleeves and lower sides. Belt is tasseled front and back. WOMEN'S SIZES: 34 to 46 bust.
LENGTH: about 46 inches. State actual bust measure
10 C 66—Medium Brown, self color embroidery.
10 C 68—Navy Blue, black embroidery.
10 C 69—Black, black embroidery.
PRICE, Postage, 16c extra $29.50

10 C 62 An inexpensive, practical Coat of warm Wool Mixed Velour coating. Flare back, two pockets and an embroidered collar. Self belt. Half lined with durable Twill. WOMEN'S SIZES: 34 to 46 bust.
LENGTH: about 46 inches. State actual bust measure
10 C 62—Medium Brown.
10 C 64—Navy Blue.
PRICE, Postage, 16c extra $8.98

10 C 70 Expertly tailored Polo Coat of warm All Wool coating. Trimmed with stitching and buttons. Large, warm convertible collar. Two pockets. Half Satteen lined. WOMEN'S SIZES: 34 to 46 bust.
LENGTH: about 46 inches. State actual bust measure
10 C 70—Reindeer Tan.
10 C 72—Navy Blue.
PRICE, Postage, 16c extra $15.98

10 C 58 Particularly handsome model of heavy All Wool coating of soft texture. Large convertible collar, cuffs and lower band of rich Caracul fur fabric. Full lined with Venetian. Wide sleeves with inner wristlets shirred on elastic. Two slot pockets. WOMEN'S SIZES: 34 to 46 bust. LENGTH: about 46 inches. State size.
10 C 58—Medium Brown.
10 C 60—Navy Blue.
PRICE, Postage, 16c extra $17.98

Your new Ward's Coat will be backed by our guarantee of satisfaction

PLATE 72. ORIGINAL W.R.T. PRINT 4" × 5"

fashion plates representative of each decade between 1910 and the 1940s. Plate 72 is indicative of the teens, while plate 73 shows a family of the 1920s or 1930s; plate 74 (made in 1947) and plate 51 are fine examples of the fashions of the 1940s.

Also found among Trivett's photographs are suggestions of the influence of the most pervasive promulgators of modern American popular culture—motion pictures and the radio. The influence of the highly popular gangster movies of the 1930s seems to have been the inspiration for the pose of the three young men in plate 75. They might as well have been three toughs from Chicago. Plate 76 also has the same Hollywoodesque "roaring twenties" feel.

Other of Trivett's photos reveal the rural/antique versus modern/mass-

Opposite page: FIGURE 3.1.
From Montgomery Ward's 1922 catalog.

PLATE 73

Seated, left to right: Clyde Bunton, Ruth Farthing Bunton. Standing, left to right: Andy Bunton, Doris Young Bunton.

market dichotomy so prevalent in 20th century Appalachia. Notice the juxtaposition (which may or may not have been intentional on the part of Trivett) in plate 77 of the man dressed in the stylish sweater with tie, belt, and jodhpurs and boots standing in front of the window with the oil lamp in it. If the man and his family did not have electricity (and many residences in Beech Mountain did not until the early 1940s), he nevertheless was not behind the times in his style of dress. Plate 78 is a very interesting photograph in this respect. The woman seated in the cane-backed chair holds a homemade banjo made by W. R. Trivett.[103] Yet along with these

PLATE 74

Theodocia Guy and Claudia Trivett, ca. 1947

icons of folk-craft can also be seen in the upper left and right hand corners of the picture two mass produced signs. The one in the right-hand corner is a thermometer advertising extracts (probably as a key ingredient for a patent medicine). The other sign, only partially shown, is intriguing. At the top of the sign only the large letter "E" can be seen. Below, the words "The Outlaw" can be read. Although unreadable in plate 78, the word below "The Outlaw" is "Loose," which can be seen in an original

Plate 75

Plate 76. Original W.R.T. print 5½" × 3¼"

PLATE 77

print of a ca. 1932 portrait of Mertie Trivett taken in the same location—
which happened to be W. R. and Mertie Trivett's front porch (see page 19).
The sign is framed in a silver, metal frame, the same type used by movie
theaters and other public establishments for advertising. What could have
Trivett been advertising on his front porch? It has been suggested by one
of W. R. Trivett's step-grandchildren that the sign was perhaps an
advertisement from a movie theater in nearby Butler, Tennessee, which
Trivett's son, Haskell, may have gotten as a souvenir. Would that Trivett

PLATE 78

Audry Guy Estep, Francis Guy Estep, ca. 1932

had included more of the sign in the picture! But he was not taking photographs to help prove future historians' theses about the modernity of Appalachian America in the first half of the 20th century. To him the mass produced signs on his front porch were nothing special or extraordinary, and did not take precedence over his main subject—his sitters.

*   *   *

W. R. Trivett's photographs reveal a wealth of information about the lives and times of his subjects. From his portraits of church groups one can view at once the socioeconomic makeup of the Flat Springs community in the late 1920s (see plate 79 of the congregation of the Flat Springs Baptist Church of Christ).[104] Note that there are men in suits, men in overalls,

PLATE 79. ORIGINAL W.R.T. PRINT 5½" × 3¼"

Congregation of Flat Springs Baptist Church of Christ, ca. 1928-29.

men in suit jackets and overalls, men with ties and slacks; they are not all poor, aged, or illiterate—as evidenced by those holding songbooks and bibles. Plates 80–83 are portraits of the mountain upper class (or at least people affecting to look like the upper class). Their suits attest to their financial security, and the pencils and pens in their coat pockets are subtle indicators of their literacy and erudition.[105] Yet it was not just the mountain elite who were proud of their ability to read and write. Plate 84 shows a man in overalls with a pencil in his bib pocket.

Most significantly, Trivett's photographs graphically tell of the mountain people's view of the land and themselves. Often Trivett used the natural scenery of the area as a backdrop for his portraits. Perhaps none of Trivett's pictures better illustrates his use of the mountain landscape to enhance the image of his sitters as plates 82 and 85. In plate 82 four stylishly dressed women of the late 1920s or early 1930s pose amidst the austere beauty of the mountain fall or winter. Plate 85 depicts a mountain family dressed in a rather cosmopolitan manner before a bucolic setting complete with ancient boulders and rustic split-rail fence. These two photographs can be interpreted negatively, that is to say as pictures meant to show the sitters' civility in spite of their backwoods surroundings. Yet the

PLATE 82

Opposite page, left: PLATE 80. ORIGINAL W.R.T. PRINT 4¼ × 3¼"
  Colonel Estep, ca. 1920.
Opposite page, right: PLATE 81. ORIGINAL W.R.T. PRINT 4¼" × 3¼".

PLATE 85

Opposite page, left: PLATE 83.
Opposite page, right: PLATE 84.

PLATE 86. ORIGINAL W.R.T. PRINT 4" × 5"

PLATE 87. ORIGINAL W.R.T. PRINT 3¼" × 4¼"

Left: PLATE 88. ORIGINAL W.R.T. PRINT 5½" × 3¼"

Right: PLATE 89. ORIGINAL NEGATIVE SIZE 4¼" × 3¼"

fact that either the sitters or Trivett chose the setting for the portraits shows that they themselves viewed their surroundings positively—as lovely, beautiful, enriching.[106]

Concerning themselves, the people photographed by Trivett wanted to be portrayed positively, as typical Americans of the 20th century. For some men this meant dressing in their best pair of overalls; the ladies generally wore their newest store bought dress (see plate 86). This is a picture of a clean, decent, all-American family. Others, such as the man in plate 87, consciously strived to put forth a more urbanite appearance. He wears the tie, vest, and coat of a businessman, and the overalls of a farmer. The picture makes more sense when viewed with plates 88 and 89. Plate 88 is an original print made by W. R. Trivett from the negative which has been contact printed as plate 89. In his prints Trivett often used mats, such as the oval one shown in plate 88 to improve his compositions. Trivett probably used such a mat when printing the negative of plate 87, thus producing the formal, urbane portrait his sitter desired.

Postscript:
The *Watauga Democrat* and *Avery Advocate*

In 1889 an article in the *Watauga Democrat* listed the five main "pests" of mountain people as "1. Book agents; 2. Lightning rod agents; 3. Sewing machine agents; 4. Organ peddlers; [and] 5. [The] whiskey distiller and drinker."[1] While the whiskey distiller and drinker may presumably be considered as indigenous nuisances to the residents of Watauga County, the other four pests can be regarded as outside influences upon the mountains. Those book agents, sewing machine agents, organ peddlers, and others may have been local residents, but they were undoubtedly pestering their neighbors with solicitations to buy nationally marketed products manufactured outside of the mountains. W. R. Trivett had contemplated doing the same in 1905 under the aegis of the World Bible House mail-order company of Philadelphia. The pages of the two local newspapers of W. R. Trivett's day, the *Watauga Democrat* and the *Avery Advocate*, are full of other examples of the mountain people's contact with contemporary America, and indeed, the rest of the world. And when examined, they elaborate on the images found in Trivett's photographs.

Just a glance at the front pages of either the *Democrat* or the *Advocate* from the early 1900s through the 1930s shows that their editors were far from oblivious to national and international events. News of seemingly obscure events (to us today) regularly found their way to the front pages of both papers. In the spring of 1912 the *Democrat* printed a disturbing account of a near riot at the May Day meeting of the American Socialist

126

party in Union Square park in New York City; in September 1927 readers of the *Advocate* learned of their nation's imperialistic foreign policy in Latin America through a captioned photograph of a Nicaraguan battlefield where U. S. troops had helped to suppress insurgent rebel forces led by General Augusto Cesar Sandino.[2] On a lighter note (but perhaps no less martial in nature), in October 1927 readers of the *Advocate* found on the front page news of champion boxer Gene Tunney's successful defense of his title against former heavyweight champion Jack Dempsey.[3] And of course, both World Wars during their respective years of carnage dominated the front pages of the *Democrat* and *Advocate*.[4] The rugged mountain terrain may have delayed the coming of modern, hard surfaced roads in Avery and Watauga counties in the first two or three decades of the 20th century, but the supposed isolation of the mountains did not shelter its people from the modern worries of unstable governments, imperialism, or world war. In national affairs both great and small, the readers of the *Avery Advocate* and *Watauga Democrat* were as well informed as any other people in small town, rural America who bothered to read the newspapers.

Yet perhaps the best indicator of Avery and Watauga county residents' connection with contemporary American culture in the first half of the 20th century comes in the advertisements found within the pages of the *Advocate* and *Democrat*. The United States at the turn of the century had been a nation of consumers for nearly forty years. By the 1910s Americans were "consuming" electricity, automobiles, radios, motion pictures, manufactured clothing, and a host of other items and services. And as the *Advocate* and *Democrat* show, residents of the mountains had no less an appetite for the products of Detroit, New York, or Hollywood (regardless of whether or not they had the means to acquire them) than the rest of the nation's consumers.

As early as 1916 the *Democrat* featured ads selling automobiles and offering service for them.[5] A plethora of other modern goods were available as well: Mountain residents in 1919 need not read the *Democrat* by the light of an oil lamp; those that could afford to do so could purchase a Delco-Light electric generator from Watauga Motor Company.[6] Just like those in the rest of the nation, mountain consumers were so bombarded with the multitude of various washing machines available for purchase that in the October 13, 1927, edition of the *Avery Advocate* the editor reprinted an article prepared by the United States Department of Agriculture to help prospective buyers decide which model best suited their needs.[7] And the clothes that were being washed in these washing machines were not necessarily home-spun. A. P. Brinkley ran an ad for his Elk Park clothing store in the November 24, 1927, edition of the *Advocate* which stated:

> We have gotten in a fine lot of Dresses in all materials and of the correct new styles, just what is being worn in the large cities, and they were bought right and will go to you at prices that will shame your neighbor who goes to the city for bargains.[8]

Brinkley's customers would have been aware of the newest fashions not only through magazines and newspapers, but also through newsreels and movies shown at the Elk Park Picture Show.[9]

Finally, two separate articles in the pages of the *Avery Advocate* give voice to the latent self-image of the mountain people evoked in the photographs of W. R. Trivett. It is an image simultaneously aware of mountain stereotypes—enough so to be sensitized to the negative ones—and yet accepting of the positive image of the pioneer heritage of the modern mountaineer.

The first article, found on the front page of the September 29, 1927, edition of the *Advocate*, demonstrates the mountain residents' knowledge of the "hillbilly"—and their denial of its application to themselves. Only this time the backwards hillbilly was from Nebraska, instead of his traditional domain of the Appalachian mountains. The article was entitled "Real Cave Man Thrills Omaha," and was the story of a 70-year-old man who "had never heard of radio, motors, or air planes." Jilted at the altar some forty years past by a young bride to be, Henry F. Morris left civilization to live alone in a cave on the banks of the Platte River.[10] A newspaper reporter had coaxed him to abandon his solitude in the wilderness to take him to see the modern wonders of Omaha.

The reporter's description of Morris is a marvelous word portrait of the clichéd Appalachian mountain man:

> The cave dweller's face is covered with a heavy beard that had been disturbed only occasionally in forty years.... Ragged and grimy, it added to his generally unkempt appearance. Small piercing eyes that perpetually blinked in the strong sunlight were deep set beneath high orbital ridges and peered through heavy, overhanging eyebrows. His crowning glory was his hair.

Morris' reaction to the marvels of the 20th century were depicted comically; he shrieked "the spirits!" when he first heard a human voice over a radio, and hid under a table when photographers began taking his picture with flashbulbs. In all, Morris was viewed as a humorous, benign, oddball. That the article found its way to the front page of the *Advocate* suggests that the editor of the paper thought his readers would enjoy reading about behavior the residents of Appalachia had been associated with, and found amusing themselves. The account was amusing, however, because the majority of the *Advocate*'s readers did not view themselves as being like Morris or his traditional Appalachian ilk.

Also found on the front page of the *Advocate*, the second article proudly proclaimed contemporary mountain people's superior character, demonstrated, of all places, on the basketball court. And their eminence stemmed from their unique pioneer heritage. In March 1929 the Cranberry High girls' basketball team won the "Champions of the South" title at the Southern Girls Basketball Tournament held at Biltmore (presumably at Asheville, North Carolina).[11] The feat earned them their team picture on the front page (it was the first local picture to be printed in the *Advocate*), and a banquet in their honor at the Mountain View Motel. Yet the true significance of the event, at least to the editor of the *Advocate*, was expressed thus:

> Avery County boasts of the highest court house East of the Rocky Mountains and the best people on earth. It is peopled with the descendants of the early pioneers who blazed the trail across the continent, some of whom, attracted by the wonderful beauty and healthfulness of this region remained and became the first settlers of this mountain land. One by one many of our sons and daughters have gone out into the world outside and demonstrated their ability and fitness to cope with the people of other parts of the world. The clean, healthy, clear eyed boys and girls of our beloved mountains are the [peers] of all the world.[12]
>
> The group above have demonstrated the ability and prowess in the line of basketball.[13]

Looking past the hyperbole, the message is clear: Mountain people were fully cognizant of, active in, and indeed successful members of contemporary modern society.

Epilogue:
Appalachia Reconsidered

The photographs of W. R. Trivett present through the microcosm of the Beech Mountain community an altogether different view of Appalachia than that which is generally found in most popular and scholarly works on the region. This is not to say that the poverty, lack of education, backwardness, and isolation described in such works as *Cabins in the Laurel* did not exist. It did, and still does—to a certain degree. Yet W. R. Trivett's body of photographs show that these conditions were by no means universal throughout the mountains. Mountain people have always known this.

Yet it has only been recently that the mountain people's view of themselves have come to light through the "discovery" of the photographs of the region's itinerant picturemen. For the most part the public has only perceived Appalachia through the images of outside photographers who contrived their photos to conform to stereotypes and traditions attributed to the mountaineers. Photographers like Bayard Wootten and Doris Ulmann worked for publishers whose aim was to sell images of what the rest of Americans thought Appalachia looked like. But W. R. Trivett and the other picturemen worked for the mountain people. The picturemen's main goal was to make their pictures "good and plain," to please their sitters. For the photographs were intended to serve as reflections of precious times, people, and feelings. In essence, the images the picturemen produced were vicarious self-portraits of the mountain people. And as Trivett's photos show, the majority of people in the mountains identified themselves with other contemporary Americans. They did not see themselves as separate, strange, and out of touch with popular culture. Rather, they dressed in the "correct new styles—just what [was] being worn in the large cities"; they drove automobiles, went to movies, took part in the important political and social events of their day. They were Americans who were proud of their heritage, but who also lived very much in the present. And as the photographs of W. R. Trivett reveal, the mountain people of the 1920s and 1930s were not the same as their counterparts of the 1860s and 1870s.

Indeed, W. R. Trivett's photographs challenge the traditional view of Appalachia and its people. They force us to reevaluate the definition of the Appalachian region, to ask what really makes "Appalachia" so unique from other rural areas of the United States. Watauga and Avery counties are unquestionably within the geographical bounds of the Appalachian region. But the images found within the body of W. R. Trivett's photos pose the question as to whether the people who lived there were culturally Appalachian. There were no mine wars in either of the two counties. Moonshining (at least as evidenced in Trivett's Dark Ridge revenuers picture and the exploits of Avery Sheriff W. H. Hughes in the early 1930s) was not looked on favorably or viewed as an appropriate way to make a living. The majority of Avery and Watauga counties' residents were literate. They were rural but not backwards. Perhaps this should be the starting point to redefining what it meant (and means) to be "Appalachian."

The photographs of W. R. Trivett and the other picturemen are an excellent, invaluable source for beginning this rediscovery of the true essence of the mountains. Rather than turning to the works of professional photographic artists for their views of Appalachia's people, historians would do better to look at the obscure work of mountain farmers who took up professional photography in their spare time as a way of supplementing their income. It is in the family photo-albums of the region that "the other Appalachia"—factual Appalachia—will be separated from cabins in the laurel, hillbillies, and overflowing moonshine.

W. R. Trivett's Notebook

*   *Denotes that a line was marked through the name and amount.*

for pictures

*Linell Ward	.10¢
Charly Birad	$2.50
*Duly Romingr	.40¢
*Vane Harmon	.20¢
*A. J. Trivett	.50¢
*50 Maggie Smitheman	.50¢
*60	.50¢
*45 John Harman	.50¢
19 Thal Greene	.60¢
*50 Tax Ward	.50¢
*50 James Rominger	.80¢
*50 and made 30	
*1.75 and [d]ew me 50 yet	
*Raley Ward	[illegible]
7	
*Linell Ward	.10¢
A. L. Ward	.45¢
*pade A. L. Ward	.45¢
Sclhon Guy	.19¢
*A. L. Ward	.50¢
*Roey Trivett	.75¢
*pad A. S. Harman	.50¢
*Linel Ward	.50¢
Duey Rominger	.50¢
Roy Trivett	$1.65

*[illegible] Cannon		.05¢
*Smyth Trivett		.07¢
*D. L. Trivett pade		.50¢
*R. J. Pamer	.04¢	.05¢

[page 2]

*loan [illegible] Ward		$1.15
*M. P. Trivett		.25¢
*pade tom Millsap		.50¢
James Romingr		.75¢
*A. L. Ward		.75¢
*Council Ward		.25¢
*Council Ward		.25¢
*Carl Trivett	$2.00	.30¢
*Carl Trivett	12	40
*Carl Trivett		25
*Carl Trivett		50

[page 3]

*Work for Anglie Dyer
*6½ hour one day
*and tow hour and ½
one day

Willie Trivett
Mertie Trivett

       Rominger,
         N. C.

[page 4]

Johny Ward due me
     .15¢

*Mail pade	5 ca
*Dandly pade	.05¢

[page 5]

*Julis Warker
for pictures   .68¢
    Paid
*Bettie Harman

$2.89
Balance due her $12.11

[page 7]

6 post cards	.15¢
30 post cards	75
5 plates	50

[page 8]

[Trivett's son, Haskell, apparently found the notebook when he was a child, hence the following writings.]

Rob Miller
And me
Haskell
Trivett
Whaley
     N. C.
     here goes a dog,
     he is after a rabbit,
     he will catch, the rabbit,

[page 9]

*John W. Ward
*due me $1.20

*last bunch pade

*paid Martha Trivett, $1.00

[page 10]

John Ward		
Due me for pictures	[illegible]	.05¢
pade	$1.00	.10¢
pade		.50¢
Develop		.15¢
6 post cards		.20¢
6 post cards		.20¢
16 3¼ × 4¼ prints		.48¢
6 large Post cards		.18¢
6 small post card		.14¢

paid	.30¢
paid	$1.50¢
6 Post cards	50
11 3¼ × 4¼ prints	44
one Roll Films	.08¢
6 3¼ × 4¼ prinds	.23¢
one Roll Film	.08¢

[page 11]

Secret Club nembers

Frankie Green
George Ward
Luella Phillips
Gladys Phillips
Faye Guy
Anna Guy

[page 86]

January, 1915		$3.17
		Eggs sold in
Eggs,	1½ doz. at 25cts. a doz.	Jan.
"	1 doz. and 9 eggs at .24¢ a doz.	42
	5 doz. and 10 " "	$1.40
	1 half doz. " at .20¢ a day	10
Butter,	2 lbs. an 1 of. at 16cts lbd.	33
"	1 lb. 10oz.	26
Eggs,	4 doz. at 22cts a doz.	88
Feb. 3	" and 10 " "	85
Eggs	1 doz. and a half at 20cts	30
	12 doz. at 15cts a d.	$1.80
Chickens 2 at 10cts a lb		93
Eggs	8 doz. and 10, at 16cts. a d.	$1.32
"	2 doz. at 13 cts a doz.	26
March	5 doz. and 9 at 14cts.	81
Eggs,	14 doz. and 10 at 12cts.	$1.78
Chicken 6 hens at 10cts a lb.		$2.25
Eggs	8-doz. and 6 at 12cts a doz.	$1.02

[page 88]

Pearl Eller	Vilas N.C.
Ed mathison	Vilas N.C.

A D Romingr   .85¢

Jan. 1915.
Mr. Smyth Trivett
*develop 17 post card
*and 3 plates   .20¢

When this you see
Think of me/tho many
miles apart we may be
W R Trivette
Mertie Trivette

Chapter Notes

Chapter I. Willie

1. According to his delayed certificate of birth registration, W. R. Trivett's legal name was Willie Roby Trivett. *Vital Statistics: Delayed Births, Watauga County Vol. 9* (Boone, North Carolina: Watauga County Court House, Register of Deeds), 418.

2. "Obituaries," *Avery Journal*, 11 August 1966.

3. Susie Guy Trivett, W. R. Trivett's daughter-in-law, interview by author, 22 June 1995, Flat Springs, North Carolina, tape recording; Auborn W. Trivett, W. R. Trivett's nephew, interview by author, 16 July 1996, Sugar Grove, North Carolina, tape recording; Ottie Greene, best friend of Haskell Trivett, W. R. Trivett's son, interview by author, 21 July 1996, Flat Springs, North Carolina, tape recording.

4. The spelling of Goulder Trivett's first name varies from census to census, and from his death certificate. In one it is spelled "Gulder," in another "Gouler"; I have chosen to use the third alternate spelling—"Goulder," from his death certificate, found in the *Index to Vital Statistics: Deaths, A–Z Watauga County* (Boone, North Carolina: Watauga County Court House, Register of Deeds).

5. Carl A. Ross, Jr., ed., *The 1870 Census of Watauga County, North Carolina* (Boone, North Carolina: Department of History, Appalachian State University, 1982), 70–71; *The 1880 Census of Watauga County, North Carolina* (Boone, North Carolina: Department of History, Appalachian State University, 1983), 114; and *Index to Vital Statistics: Deaths, A–Z Watauga County.*

6. Carl A. Ross, Jr., ed., *The 1900 Census of Watauga County, North Carolina* vol. 2 (Boone, North Carolina: Department of History, Appalachian State University, 1984), 297.

7. Carl A. Ross, Jr., ed., *The 1910 Census of Watauga County, North Carolina* vol. 2 (Boone, North Carolina: Department of History, Appalachian State University, 1986), 279–280; and *1900 Census of Watauga County,* 297.

8. Auborn Trivett, interview by author, 16 July 1996; and Sanna Ross Gaffney et al., *The Heritage of Watauga County, North Carolina* vol. 1 (Winston-Salem,

North Carolina: Heritage of Watauga County Book Committee in cooperation with the History Division of Hunter Publishing Co., 1984), 54.

9. W. Paul Bingham, "The Growth and Development of Education in Watauga County" (Master's thesis, Appalachian State Teachers College, 1950), 84. The period between 1900 and 1920 saw a dramatic increase in school attendance in Watauga County. In 1901 the average daily attendance was 2,101, while that of 1920 was 3,224—an increase from 56 percent to 84 percent. (88)

10. Reka W. Shoemake et al., *Development of Public Education in Watauga County, North Carolina* compiled by a Bicentennial Committee (Boone, North Carolina: Appalachian State University, 1976), 13.

11. Gaffney et al. 54. As many as ten schools were located in the area in the late 19th and early 20th centuries. This included the Zion Colored School, formed in 1882. (53)

12. Bessie Willis Hoyt, *Come When the Timber Turns* (Banner Elk, North Carolina: Pudding Stone Press, 1983), 162. This quote is taken from an account written by Martha Ellen Church (1871–1951), and reprinted by Hoyt in her book, pp. 159–162.

13. Daniel J. Whitener, *Story of Watauga County: A Souvenir of Watauga Centennial* (Boone, North Carolina: Town of Boone, 1949), 64.

14. Bingham 72.

15. Whitener 67.

16. Whitener 65.

17. Bingham 88.

18. Bingham 76. There were also 169 thirteen year olds, 147 fourteen year olds, 157 fifteen year olds, 125 sixteen year olds, 93 seventeen year olds, 79 eighteen year olds, 45 nineteen year olds, and 47 twenty year olds attending Watauga County Schools. (76)

19. Bingham 76.

20. Whitener 65. These books were recommended by the Board of Public Instruction in 1898. (65)

21. Bingham 77.

22. Hoyt 122.

23. Hoyt 126.

24. W. R. Trivett papers [photocopy] (henceforth referred to as WRTP) in possession of the author by permission of Susie Guy Trivett, Flat Springs, North Carolina. The Linville River Lumber Company was the subsidiary of the Linville River Railroad Company, which serviced the Pineola Lumber and Trading Company in the late 19th century. Sometime after the turn of the century both companies went into receivership, and were bought by Isaac T. Mann of Bramwell, West Virginia. Mann eventually sold the companies to the W. M. Ritter Lumber Company. (John Preston Arthur, *Western North Carolina: A History 1730–1913*, Raleigh, North Carolina: Edwards & Broughton Printing Company, 1914; reprint, Spartanburg, South Carolina: The Reprint Company, 1973, pp. 482–83.)

25. WRTP, W. M. Ritter Lumber Co. and Linville River Lumber Co. pay envelope, February 1906 and May 1907.

26. *1920 North Carolina Census: Avery County, Vol. 6: Beech Mountain Township* (Washington, D. C.: National Archives). Trivett's servant was an illiterate

white male 16 years old. He was paid "on account." It is likely he was hired to help Trivett's wife with their 15 month old son, Haskell. Trivett's daughter-in-law, Susie G. Trivett, has stated that Trivett's wife had a difficult pregnancy, and therefore may have needed help with her chores.

27. Susie Guy Trivett, interview by author, 22 June 1995; Auborn W. Trivett, interview by author, 16 July 1996; and Ottie Greene, interview by author, 21 July 1996.

28. The typed paper in Trivett's collection states the following:

State of North Carolina,
Avery County,

I, W. H. Hughes, Sheriff of Avery County, North Carolina, have this day appointed Willie Trivett, Deputy Sheriff, for Avery County, North Carolina, this appointment to remain in full force and effect until otherwise revoked.

This December 3rd, 1934
[signed],
W. H. Hughes, Sheriff

29. WRTP, National Youth Administration letter to W. R. Trivett, 29 October 1937. The area known as Whaley, North Carolina, is approximately only two or three miles from the area known as Flat Springs, North Carolina, where W. R. Trivett lived. Often the name "Whaley" has been used for the entire area of Flat Springs, and vice versa.

30. WRTP, National Youth Administration postcard to Haskell Trivett, 20 July 1940. This may or may not indicate that W. R. Trivett and his family were receiving federal relief at this time during the Depression. At the inception of its creation in June 1935, the National Youth Administration employed only those youth whose "families were certified for relief, with employment based on the individual degree of destitution." However, in November 1939, in an effort to more effectively reach all youth who needed work experience in North Carolina, NYA authorities were authorized to employ "up to 15 percent of the total youth employment in the state on the basis of training needs." (The National Archives and National Archives and Records Service, General Services Administration, *Selected Records of the National Youth Administration Relating to North Carolina 1935–1943* Record Group 119, records of the National Youth Administration, Washington, D. C.: The National Archives, 1984, microfilm, pp. 4 and 16.)

31. *Selected Records of the NYA* 4.

32. *Selected Records of the NYA* 4–5.

33. *Selected Records of the NYA* 55.

34. *Selected Records of the NYA* 55.

35. *The Watauga Democrat*, 22 April; 25 February; and 16 December 1937.

36. *Selected Records of the NYA* 81. The time and place is not given, nor can be found in the *Avery Advocate* or *Watauga Democrat*.

37. The postcard sent to Haskell Trivett states: [typed]

Dear Mr. Trivett:

Please report for work, Monday morning, July 29, at the old school building at Whaley N.C.

> Sincerely,
> [signed]
> Herbert B. Gray
> NYA County Supervisor

[written]
Come as soon as you get this card and wait there for me.

Perhaps Haskell Trivett was transported from the Whaley school to work on another project somewhere else in the county.

38. WRTP, World Bible House letter to W. R. Trivett, 10 May 1905.

39. WRTP, World Bible House letter, 1905.

40. WRTP, World Bible House letter, 1905. The letter was dictated.

41. WRTP, World Bible House letter, 1905.

42. WRTP, "Dots and Dashes," Published Quarterly in the Interest of Ambitious Young Men and Women, by the Southern School of Telegraphy, July 1909.

43. WRTP, "Dots and Dashes."

44. WRTP, The Ransomerian School of Penmanship letters to W. R. Trivett, November 26, 1909, and February 10, 1910.

45. WRTP, The Ransomerian School letters.

46. WRTP, W. R. Trivett to Mertie Weaver, 16 April 1911.

47. Ross, *1910 Census of Watauga County* 277, and Terry L. Harmon, *The Harmon Family 1670–1984: The Genealogy of Cutliff Harmon and His Descendants* vol. 1 (Boone, North Carolina: Terry L. Harmon, 1984), 209.

48. WRTP, Ethel Weaver, to Mertie Weaver, 6 March 1911.

49. It is likely that Weaver copied this poem around 1906–09; most of her extant letters date from this time. The Victorian code of womanhood lasted over a decade after the monarch's death in 1901, and was put to rest only after the First World War.

50. WRTP, undated writing by Mertie Weaver.

51. Conversation with Linda Clawson, W. R. Trivett's step-granddaughter, 27 November 1997; conversation with Susie Guy Trivett, 4 December 1997; conversation with Deloris Guy Lentz, W. R. Trivett's step-granddaughter, 4 December 1997.

52. See WRTP, Mertie Weaver's postcards to W. R. Trivett, March 17, 1908, through December 1911.

53. WRTP, Mertie Weaver, to W. R. Trivett, 10 October 1909. On the back of one of her calling cards Weaver also wrote:

> "Dear Willie"
>
> "Days may pass and
> weeks may End,
> But still you will
> find me your own
> true love forever,"
> x x
>
> Mertie,

It was not long before Trivett's friends began associating him and Weaver as a couple deeply in love. In a June 1909 postcard sent to Trivett, a friend of his wrote, "Say Luck why didn't you come to see *Miss Trivett* Sunday? I will tell you she is [quite] mad. you must be sure that you see Miss Trivett Sunday now of course you no who I mean..." Charley Trivett, who evidently frequently courted his own sweetheart along with Weaver and W. R. Trivett on Sundays, chided Trivett in the same manner:

> Mr. Willie Harmon [or] Weaver [or] Trivett I mean ... Say now Willie you come home as soon as you can Mrs. Harmon Said to Tell you to come and come quick for Mertie is sick, ha ha[.]
>
> Willie I have Been to see my Sweet Darling little girl ever Sunday sence you have been gone and if Sunday was to come two times a week [I] would go to see her... I have saw Mertie Ever Sunday sence you have Been gone—if you Ever want to see Mertie any more you had Better come Back[.] you wouldn't hardly know her now she has Been [trembling] so she stays at home just like a old woman. you had Better come and [Receive]? her...
>
> Well will you write and tell me when you are coming [I] have come [to] miss you affel Bad But not as Bad as Mertie does[.] now I mean what I say come home[.] I guess you are in Mountain City Jail ho ho[.] John Phillips is in there[.] Bye Bye ans Real Soon and tell me when you are coming Back.

> Charley Trivett
> Yours Truely

(WRTP, Charley Trivett, to W. R. Trivett, 26 April 1911.) W. R. Trivett was working during this time in Southerland, Tennessee, and stayed there until the fourth Sunday in May. See WRTP, Goulder Trivett, to W. R. Trivett, 19 April 1911, and W. R. Trivett, to Mertie Weaver, 16 April 1911.

54. There are in Trivett's papers two small photographs of a pair of attractive young ladies of the turn of the century—Daisy Keller and Etter Keller, respectively. It appears Trivett risked the peril of courting two sisters.

55. *Index to Marriages from 1873–1974 L–Z, Watauga County* (Boone, North Carolina: Watauga County Courthouse, Register of Deeds).

56. Harmon 89. The 1910 census of Watauga County shows that Mertie Weaver lived with W. M. and Elizabeth Harmon; she was listed as a servant. (Ross 60.)

57. WRTP, W. M. and Elizabeth Harmon will, 12 September 1927.

58. Ross, *1900 Census of Watauga County* vol. 2, 63. W. M. Harmon's occupation is listed as "Farmer/Miller." Susie Guy Trivett recalls that Harmon moved the location of his store at least twice. The first store he had was on Beech Mountain; the second was located in Flat Springs.

59. WRTP, see W. M. Harmon's 1896 notebook, "Dry Goods, and Groceries" notebook from 1926, "Pierce's Memorandum and Account Book" (there are several of these dating from 1896 to 1910), and correspondence from the National Remedy Company, Manufacturing Chemists, Proprietary Medicines of New York. Harmon also ordered patent medicines from the Gypsy Remedy Co. of New York as well. This included 12 bottles of Gypsy Magic Oil, 6 bottles of Herb Compound and Blood Purifier, and 12 bottles of Little Liver Pills. (Gypsy Remedy Co., invoice, 13 November 1900.)

60. WRTP, Hall of Snow, Lodge No. 363 bill for dues, 5 June 1916, and the Beery Correspondence School of Horsemanship letter to W. M. Harmon, 3 June 1918.

61. WRTP, see *Avery County Book of Deeds* (Newland, North Carolina: Avery County Courthouse, Register of Deeds), Book 10, p. 294, and Book 20, p. 276. Harmon was also somewhat litigious in nature. In 1926 he filed suit against E. C. Harmon and H. L. Weaver—his son-in-law and Mertie Trivett's father—for the sum of $709.83. (See WRTP, Butler & Grayson, Attorneys at Law, Mountain City, Tennessee, letter to W. M. Harmon, 30 January 1926.)

62. Susie Guy Trivett has stated that W. R. and Mertie Trivett lived in at least two different places in Flat Springs before moving into the Harmons' house.

63. *Avery County Deeds* Book 10, 294.

64. The deed states:

> ...we Willie Trivett + Mertie Trivett do Hereby agree and Promise To take care and surport the said W. M. Harmon and Bettie [Elizabeth] Harmon and stay with Same, through all sickness and care for Same Until Death Seprate us all.

The Harmons in their 1927 will left Mertie Trivett

> all our house hold goods and Kitchen furniture. All domestic fowls and poultery . One Red cow 3 years old one mowing mechine. one hay Rake and all other farming Tools. One Wagon. with bed. all money notes and Bonds on hand at our deaths.

It was also stipulated that Mertie Trivett was to divide the estate with her mother, Sallie Weaver, however she (Mertie Trivett) wished. (WRTP, Harmon will, 12 September 1927.)

65. Hoyt 58. Hoyt recalled after sitting through a scorching sermon at a church in Heaton, Avery County, that "Jonathan Edwards had nothing on this mountain preacher except a better education." (58)

66. *Minutes of the Flat Springs Baptist Church of Christ: 20 September 1902 through 18 December 1937* vol. 1 (henceforth referred to as FSBCHM), Melvin and Regina Jones, Old Beech Mountain, North Carolina, 156.

67. Susie Guy Trivett, interview by author, 22 June 1995; Auborn W. Trivett, interview by author, 16 July 1996; and Ottie Greene, interview by author, 21 July 1996.

68. FSBCHM 5. The 17 founding members of Flat Springs Baptist Church were: W. F. Jones, Edonton Mitchell, A. C. Johnson, J. R. Green, B. C. Green, S. M. Green, W. E. Trivett, Charley York, Mary Jones, Lucinda Reece, Nancy Mitchell, Julie Johnson, Grace Johnson, Violett Green, Kisah York, Hannah Green, and Cardelia York. (5) They subscribed to the following Articles of Faith:

> 1. We believe in one only true and living God that there are three persons in the god head the Father and the Son and the Holy Ghost and these three are one in substance, equal in power and glory.
> 2. We believe the doctrine of original sin.
> 3. We believe in Scriptures of the old and new testament being the Word of God and only for our faith and practice.

4. We believe that sinners are justified in the sight of God only by the imputed righteousness of Jesus Christ.

5. We believe that the Saints shall persevere in grace and that by so doing they never finally fall away.

6. We believe that Baptism and the Lord's supper are ordinances instituted by Christ and that true believers are the only proper subjects there of.

7. We believe that the only time an apostolic made of baptism is by immersion in the water.

8. We believe in the resurrection from the dead and a general judgment and that the punishment of the wicked shall be everlasting and the joys of the righteous eternal.

9. We now the members of the Baptist Church of Christ at Flat Springs agreeing to these articles of faith do covenant and give ourselves up in prayer to God for each other that they may grow in grace and knowledge of our Lord and Savior Jesus Christ. [1]

69. In book I of the minutes of Flat Springs Baptist Church, 1902–1937, see pp. 21, 26, 43, 49, 51, 67, 118, 125, 145, 169, 209, and 217.

70. FSBCHM 189, 203.

71. See Flat Springs Baptist Church minute book I, 237; and Flat Springs Baptist Church minute book II, 1938–1973, 20, 45, 85, 104, 134, 182. In addition to this, Trivett was often called to pray during services, as well as give the benediction.

72. Mertie Trivett was also appointed on three separate occasions to speak with wayward members. See minute book I, 222; and minute book II, 32 and 68.

73. I have used a fictitious name for the offending member.

74. J. M. Harmon, church clerk, recorded Trivett's plea:

Bro W. R. Trivett made his report of [Eugene Guy] and said that he talked to him and he said that he did not want the church to withdraw fellowship from him by motion to give him another month to come and make his acknowledgment to the church. [FSBCHM book I, 68]

75. FSBCHM book II, 26 January 1946, 69.

76. FSBCHM book II 69.

77. If the first three decades of Flat Springs Baptist Church's history (as recorded in its first minute book, 1902–1937) was one of judgment, the following four decades were ones of grace. The second minute book, 1937–1973, is filled mostly with accounts of revivals, the winning of souls, and only an occasional excommunication. (The last citing of a withdrawal of fellowship was made on January 31, 1952.) Indicative of this change was pastor Lawrence Hagaman's suggestion on 4 December 1948 for all the Sunday School classes to study repentance, baptism, and the Lord's supper, and for the Baptist Training Union to study grace and faith. (FSBCHM book II, 99)

Chapter II. Willie R. Trivett, Photographer

1. William Welling, *Photography in America: The Formative Years 1839–1900* (New York: Thomas Y. Crowell, 1978), 8, and Helmut Gernsheim and Allison Gernsheim, *The History of Photography, From the Earliest Use of the Camera Obscura in the Eleventh Century Up to 1914* (London, New York, Toronto: Geoffrey Cumberlege, Oxford University Press, 1955), 56. The Gernsheims' stated that "Perhaps no other invention ever captured the imagination of the public to such a degree and conquered the world with such lightning rapidity as the daguerreotype." (56)

2. Welling 17, and Gernsheim 170. Tintypes "were collected in albums, or cut to any shape or size and fitted into brooches, lockets, shirt studs, &c." (Gernsheim 170)

3. Welling 117. Anywhere from four to 36 images could be produced at one time. Of course, the more images there were on one plate, the tinnier they were. Images from a 36 image plate were called "gem" tintypes. (117)

4. Welling 158. Camp photographers were more prevalent in the Union armies; as the war turned against the South, and silver, nitrate, and money became ever more precious and scarce in the Confederacy, Southern photographers became even rarer. As was stated at the time, Southern photographers had "nothing to work with, and nobody to work for, and, probably, are forced to go soldiering." (169)

5. John Szarkowski, *Photography Until Now* (New York; Boston; Toronto: The Museum of Modern Art, 1989), 125.

6. Szarkowski 125. Eastman built on the work of two English amateur photographers, Dr. Richard Leach Maddox and Charles Harper Bennett, both of whom were instrumental in the development of dry plate negatives.

7. Szarkowski 127, 131. It has been estimated that a photographer working in the field with wet plates was fortunate to make six plates a day.

8. Szarkowski 125–26.

9. Szarkowski 141.

10. Szarkowski 141.

11. Beaumont Newhall, *The History of Photography from 1839 to the Present Day* (New York: The Museum of Modern Art, 1949), 112.

12. Newhall 112.

13. Welling 345.

14. Szarkowski 144.

15. Szarkowski 151.

16. David Moltke-Hansen, "Seeing the Highlands, 1900–1939: Southwestern Virginia Through the Lens of T. R. Phelps," *Southern Cultures* vol. 1, no. 1, 1994, 24.

17. Moltke-Hansen 23, 24.

18. I am assuming that A. J. Campbell was a man; for all I know, however, "A. J." could have stood for "Alice Jane."

19. *Watauga Democrat*, 26 September 1918.

20. "Photo Shop Now in Improved Quarters," *Watauga Democrat*, 24 June 1937, 1. The ad stated:

> Mr. Paul Weston announces the removal of his Boone Photo Shop to the Jones building, opposite the Belk-White Co., and the establishment has been enlarged, modernized and improved to the point where it is one of the best studios in this section of the state.
>
> Mr. Weston, who had four years experience with MGM in Hollywood, and two years with a New York studio before coming to Boone, has enjoyed splendid patronage here. [1]

Implicit in the references to Hollywood and New York is that Mr. Weston made his subjects look glamorous or cosmopolitan.

21. Buchanan never mentioned meeting Trivett.

22. Ann Hawthorne, ed., *The Picture Man* photographs by Paul Buchanan, with foreword and introduction by Bruce Morton (Chapel Hill: The University of North Carolina Press, 1993), xvii.

23. Hawthorne xvii. Paul Buchanan inherited his father's cameras and enlarger (Fate Buchanan was a photographer as well), but he never used the enlarger. (104, 118) Buchanan mentioned that his father did experiment with the use of a flash; yet the younger Buchanan was apparently not impressed with his father's application of artificial lighting. He stated:

> ...now my daddy, he used [a flash] a lot. But I never did. I guess he was mostly wanting to try it out. See how it worked. He got us out one night late in the evening—might have been after dark—made our picture. It made the funniest looking picture ever was. I reckon some of us jumped. It didn't do right at all. [122]

24. This was very profitable for Buchanan. For a picture that cost him 80 cents to have enlarged, he charged $4.50. (118)

25. Hawthorne 108.

26. Hawthorne 126.

27. Hawthorne 126.

28. Edited at various times by Frank Carr, Frank B. Schumann, Kelly Hagie, and Carl D. Osborne, the *Avery Advocate* enjoyed a limited circulation from 1926 through 1937. Horton Cooper, *History of Avery County, North Carolina* (Asheville, NC: Biltmore Press, 1964), 55.

29. *Avery Advocate*, 6 October 1927. Frank A. Carr was editor.

30. "New Photo Studio," *Avery Advocate*, 10 January 1929, 1.

31. "The New Studio," *Avery Advocate*, 7 February 1929. The *Advocate* stated: "The Tip Top Studio opened Monday over the Advocate office and is being kept busy and receiving praise for its work. Notice their advertisement this week extending the time for a free enlargement."

32. Tip Top Studio ads, *Avery Advocate*, 7, 14, February 1929.

33. "The Tip Top Studio," *Avery Advocate*, 4 April 1929.

34. "Kodak Troubles," *Avery Advocate*, 25 April 1929, 1.

35. "Avery Advocate Now Being Published by New Owner," *Avery Advocate*, 8 May 1930, 1.

36. "The Carrs Photographers," *Avery Advocate*, 24 July 1930.

37. Susie Guy Trivett, W. R. Trivett's daughter-in-law, interview by author, 22 June 1995, Flat Springs, North Carolina.

38. W. R. Trivett papers [photocopy] (henceforth referred to as WRTP), "Sun Pictures" instructions. The instructions read:

SUN PICTURES

DIRECTIONS—Place the glossy side of print paper to dull side of negative. Put both in holder with negative side up. Hold in the sunlight with negative side up for a few minutes. In cloudy weather it takes longer. You can get extra papers at the store. This paper will also print with your Kodak films.

Made in the U. S. A.

Why not save the complete selection of Sun Pictures, there are 144 subjects.

39. WRTP, Conley Camera Company guarantee for camera No. S82768. This is the only camera guarantee found among Trivett's papers. That Trivett cared enough to save it suggests that it meant something to him—that it was his first camera.

40. The Conley Camera Company, *Catalog No. 5, Cameras, Silent Shutters and Photographic Apparatus* (Rochester, Minnesota: The Conley Camera Company, ca. 1911–1913). The company also sold a number of silent shutters, which eliminated the "click" of making an exposure. "Every one that has ever posed for a picture knows what a trying moment it is when the shutter clicks," stated the catalog's author.

> Do your best and you are unable to conceal that nervous attack that creeps over one, and that is why so many failures occur.... Every photographer fully appreciates what it means to have absolute silence the instant he makes an exposure. That is what a Silent Shutter does for the man that wants a down-to-date instrument. [29]

41. Susie Guy Trivett, interview by author, 22 June 1995.

42. *The Focal Encyclopedia of Photography* (New York: The MacMillan Company, 1960), 1250.

43. The Conley Camera Company offered only two view cameras in its No. 5 catalog—the Queen City View Cameras No. 38 and No. 40. In the 5 × 7 size, (which is the size that Trivett most probably ordered, for this gave him the option of also using other, smaller size plates, such as 3¼ × 5½, No. 40 with the "Regno Double Valve Shutter and R. R. Lens" started at $26. (27) No. 38, in its most regal configuration with "Autex Shutter and Lens Series V. F.6.8 Anastigmat Lens," cost $72. (25)

44. WRTP, see Montgomery Ward & Co. to W. R. Trivett, 7 August 1908; John M. Smyth Co. to W. R. Trivett, 15 September 1908; and W. R. Trivett to Mess. Wehman Brothers, 7 May 1909. In this last letter Trivett affected a more professional appearance by signing his name "Yours respectfully, William Trivett." This is the only surviving document in which Trivett ever signed his name in this manner. Trivett also ordered photographic supplies from more local dealers, as a letter from Cargille's Art Gallery of Johnson City, Tennessee, dated 8 October 1907 attests.

45. *The Southeastern Photo News* was mostly an advertising vehicle for the Atlanta Photo Supply Co., but in the October 1934 issue it did have some rather interesting articles/editorials on the New Deal. Professional photographers' status within the Codes of the NRA was the particular concern of an article by Robert R. Jennings, president of the Georgia Photographers Association. In the article Jennings passed along news of the change of code classification for professional photographers. It was a change long due in Jennings' estimation:

> Since the last issue of *The Photo News*, our Code has been located definitely under Division 2 of the NRA.... This means that Photography has been definitely recognized by the Government that we have a product to make and deliver as well as a service to perform for the public.
>
> I may say here for some time that it has been beyond my comprehension and every reason that I have had at my command to understand why our Code was ever placed under Division 5, which is purely a Service Division for bootblacks, cleaning and pressing, restaurants and hotels, hat cleaners and others; for when a patron comes into a studio, before they can be completely served, they must walk out of the studio with a processed and made product. [5]

46. "Making pictures" is the term most often used by those who knew Trivett to describe his work as a photographer.

47. Over the years Trivett changed the address of the stamp as the name of the region he lived in changed; "Whaley" later became "Beech Creek," and "Beech Creek" in turn became "Flat Springs."

48. WRTP, Lilly Reese to W. R. Trivett, 28 December 1909.

49. WRTP, John Rominger to W. R. Trivett, 1910.

50. Susie Guy Trivett, interview by author, 22 June 1995.

51. Viola Ward Guy, interview by author, 17 October 1997, Flat Springs, North Carolina, tape recording, in possession of author. Guy and her family were photographed many times by Trivett. She recalled that he was well known within the Flat Springs community for his "picture making business," and that most people came to his house to have their picture taken.

52. WRTP, Custer Ward to W. R. Trivett, 12 June 1910. Ward wrote:

> Dear Sir they is quite a lot of pictures to be taken up here and I want you to come and take my father and mother so come and you can get enough work to pay for your trip So I will tell ever body that you will be here. So come the 22 June yours truly
>
> Custer Ward

53. WRTP, W. R. Trivett's notebook, ca. 1914–January 1915. The twenty people who paid for photographs have a line drawn through their name and the amount; I am assuming that this denotes that they had paid Trivett for the pictures. See appendix for a copy of the notebook (transcribed).

54. WRTP, Trivett's notebook. This is a conservative estimate based on Trivett's figures.

55. See appendix. The cost of developing prints depended on which brand/

type of paper, chemicals, and plates Trivett used. He also recorded making six postcards for 50 cents, or 8 cents per card.

56. The profit percentage is derived by dividing Trivett's profit, 32 cents, by what he charged, 80 cents.

57. See appendix. By my calculations he actually made $3.39.

58. Trivett worked 156 hours that month to earn a gross pay of $23.40. After deductions, however, he only took home $13.90 (WRTP, Linville River Lumber Co. pay envelope, May 1907).

59. As defined in Robert Isbell's *The Last Chivaree: The Hicks Family of Beech Mountain* foreword by Wilma Dykeman (Chapel Hill: The University of North Carolina Press, 1996).

60. Viola Ward Guy, interview by author, 17 October 1997. This picture was identified by Guy who was also baptized the same day. She identified the two ministers as Dwight Edmisten and Ray Minton, of Beech Valley Baptist Church.

61. Trivett's wife and son can be found on the third row, third from the left. Haskell Trivett appears to be approximately five years old—hence the date 1923. Trivett and his family joined the church in January 1923.

62. "Stricken Appalachia," *Watauga Democrat*, 31 August 1916, 1.

63. "Watauga Storm-Swept," *Watauga Democrat*, 20 July 1916. It seems that nearly everyone in Watauga County was struck by the biblical proportions of the downpour of July 15 and 16. Z. T. Watson, writing of the damage caused by the flood in the Riverside area of the county, felt the need to close his description with a quote describing the omnipotence of God:

> Mr. Editor, I might give other particulars concerning the devastation wrought by the terrible flood, but for fear of making my article too long, I will close by quoting Gov. Bob Taylor's beautiful tribute to the power of God, which follows:
>
> I saw the awful majesty and might of Jehovah, flying on the wings of the tempest, planting His footsteps on the trackless deep, veiled in darkness and in clouds. God is everywhere and in everything. His mystery is in every bud and blossom, and leaf and tree; in every rock and hill and vale and mountain; in every stream and rivulet and river. The rustle of His wing in every Zephyr, its might in every tempest. He dwells in the dark pavilions of every storm cloud. The lightning is His messenger and the thunder His voice. His awful tread is in every earthquake and on every angry ocean; and the heavens above us teem with His myriads of shining witness; the universe of solar systems, whose wheeling orbs course the crystal paths of space, proclaim through the dread halls of eternity the glory, and power, and dominion of the all-wise, Omnipotent and Eternal God.

("Freshet Causes Much Damage at Riverside, N.C.," *Watauga Democrat*, 26 July 1916, 1.)

64. Bessie Willis Hoyt, *Come When the Timber Turns* (Banner Elk, NC: Pudding Stone Press, 1984), 125.

65. Hoyt 125.

66. "8 Stills Captured By County Officers," *Avery Advocate* 28 September 1933. Congress had voted in February 1933 to repeal Prohibition. By December the 18th Amendment had been nullified by the 21st Amendment to the Constitution.

67. See "Two Liquor Raids by Sheriff's Office," 5 Jan. 1933; "Sheriff, Deputies Get Stills, Liquor," 9 Feb. 1933; "6 Stills Taken by County Force," 20 Apr. 1933; "Copper Still, Beer Taken by Officers," 24 Aug. 1933; "8 Stills Captured by County Officers," 28 Sept. 1933; and "Sheriff Captures 2 Liquor Stills," 10 May 1934, *Avery Advocate*, front page.

68. "3 Held, One Hunted in Ambush on Hughes, Two Deputies," *Avery Advocate* 6 July 1933. Lloyd and Clarence Aldridge, and Ed Aldridge (Clarence's son), were charged with the shooting of the sheriff and his deputies. Wess Buchanan was prosecuted for being the owner of the shotgun which had been used in the "ambush" on Hughes.

69. "Sheriff W. H. Hughes Lauded for Work in Suppressing Crime," *Avery Advocate* 16 September 1933.

70. "W. P. A. Aids Road System," *Avery Advocate*, 25 February 1937, 1.

71. *Ibid.*

72. Of the 460 portraits in Trivett's collection, 104 are of children. Family portraits number 126, couples 106, and adult individual portraits 89.

73. Isbell 70.

74. Isbell 70–71.

75. By looking closely at the print of Trivett's portrait of Mitchell, one can see the faded imprint of letters which have long ago fallen off the negative that give Mitchell's name and age—112 years. Mitchell's death certificate lists his birth as January 13, 1805; he died on June 10, 1919, aged 114 years. His name is spelled on the death certificate "Eadington Mitchell," but I have chosen to use the spelling of his name as listed in the first minute book of the Flat Springs Baptist Church of Christ, September 20, 1902–December 18, 1937. *Vital Statistics: Deaths, Avery County* Vol. 1 (Newland, NC: Avery County Courthouse, Register of Deeds), 347.

76. *Minutes of the Flat Springs Baptist Church of Christ: 20 September 1902 through 18 December 1937* Book 1, Melvin and Regina Jones, Old Beech Mountain, North Carolina, 5.

77. WRTP, Carl Edmisten letters to W. R. Trivett, 6 May 1907–27 March 1910.

78. WRTP, Carl Edmisten to W. R. Trivett, 25 October 1909.

79. In the collection of Trivett's negatives are several small, plastic negatives of pictures taken in the 1950s.

80. As children my cousin and I would climb up into the loft of the wood-shed and rummage through the old trunk which held Willie's negatives. The ghost-like images on the negatives fascinated and frightened us at the same time. Often we would toss negatives out of the loft into the corn-crib below and watch with delight as they shattered into many different pieces. There is no telling how many we destroyed in that way before we finally grew old enough to know better.

Chapter III. The Photographs of W. R. Trivett and the Other Appalachia

1. Henry D. Shapiro, *Appalachia on Our Mind: The Southern Mountains and Mountaineers in the American Consciousness, 1870–1920* (Chapel Hill: The University of North Carolina Press, 1978), ix. There is research going on, however,

that asserts that the idea of "Appalachia" as being a separate region of the United States culturally, originated in the early nineteenth century.

2. Shapiro 3.

3. Shapiro 3. In his 1873 article "A Strange Land and Peculiar People," published in *Lippincott's Magazine*, Will Wallace Henry described the people he encountered in an 1869 trip through the Cumberland mountains as being

> characterized by marked peculiarities of the anatomical frame. The elongation of the bones, the contour of the facial angle, the relative proportion or disproportion of the extremities, the loose muscular attachment of the ligatures, and the harsh features were exemplified in the notable instance of the late President Lincoln. A like individuality appears in their idiom ... [which] is peculiar to the mountains, as well on the Wabash and Allegheny, I am told, as in Tennessee. [3]

4. Shapiro 4, 18.

5. Shapiro 62.

6. Shapiro 183.

7. Allen W. Batteau, *The Invention of Appalachia* (Tucson: The University of Arizona Press, 1990). Batteau asserts that

> Appalachia is a creature of the urban imagination. The folk culture, the depressed area, the romantic wilderness, the Appalachia of fiction, journalism, and public policy, have for more than a century been created, forgotten, and rediscovered, primarily by the economic opportunism, political creativity, or passing fancy of urban elites. [1]

8. Shapiro 79.

9. Shapiro 120.

10. Shapiro 17. Shapiro cites the protagonist of John Esten Cooke's "Owlet" (1878) for a description of the cultural destitution of Appalachia's residents:

> Nothing could have surprised me more than to meet these people in this hut of the Blue Ridge Mountains in Virginia, in the nineteenth century. Twenty miles from them railway trains were speeding along freighted with well dressed passengers reading the latest telegraphic news in the day's paper, and here were two beings who, as I soon found, could neither read nor write, and were destitute of all ideas beyond the wants of the human animal in the state of nature. [17]

11. Shapiro 76.

12. Charles Alan Watkins, "Merchandising the Mountaineer: Photography, the Great Depression, and *Cabins in the Laurel*," *Appalachian Journal: A Regional Studies Review* (Spring 1985): 215.

13. Sheppard relied heavily upon Jason Deyton's unpublished manuscript "The History of the Toe River Valley to 1865," as well as copies of early land grants. Other works she used were Charles Dudley Warner's *On Horseback: A Tour in Virginia, North Carolina, and Tennessee* (1888), and Olive Dame Campbell and Cecil J. Sharp's *English Folk Songs from the Southern Appalachians* (1917). These works, along with her use of court documents and voting records, lent her work an authoritative, scholarly air.

14. Watkins 217.

15. Muriel Early Sheppard, *Cabins in the Laurel*, foreword by John Ehle, 1991 ed. (Chapel Hill and London: The University of North Carolina Press, 1935, 1991). See Ehle's foreword. He views the book as Sheppard's poetic tribute to her neighbors.

16. Uncle Milt Pendley was a relative youngster at 79; Uncle Zack McHone was 90; John McNeal was 93 and a veteran of both Confederate and Union armies; Granny Silvers was 94, and Aunt Polly Boone (Daniel Boone's great-granddaughter) was reportedly "so old she [had] lost count." (46, 238, 277)

17. Sheppard 86.

18. Sheppard 131.

19. Sheppard 131. Concerning immigrant/black labor and native relations in the mountains, Sheppard wrote:

> A combination of either native and foreign or native and Negro labor is bound to prove explosive in the mountains, and things began to happen very soon. There were fights, and often murder. Usually the unaccounted-for "furriners" got the worst of it. [124]

20. Sheppard 137, 138.

21. Sheppard 153.

22. Sheppard 146.

23. Mertice M. James and Dorothy Brown, eds., *The Book Review Digest* Thirty-First Annual Cumulation, March 1935 to February 1936 Inclusive (New York: The H. W. Wilson Company, 1936), 903.

24. Watkins 232.

25. Watkins 231, 232.

26. Sheppard 131; Watkins 231, 232.

27. James and Brown, 903; Watkins 220.

28. The nostalgic patina of the 56 years between its first and second printing, however, has made *Cabins in the Laurel* a favorite of locals in the mountains today. In his 1991 foreword to the second printing of the book, novelist John Ehle stated that *Cabins* was one of the most popular books in Mitchell, Avery, and Yancey counties. He writes:

> With many converts, in many ways, in our own time the book makes its way into the minds and feelings of the people who were its subject. For them, and for those who are not relatives or natives, it offers the most friendly, easily read, vigorous, zestful portrait of Appalachians we have from the past. It is a work of affection, created for us by a shy lady and her photographer who came visiting, and were understandably chastised, and who have stayed to earn our praise. [ix]

29. James and Brown, 903, from Percy Hutchison's April 7, 1935, *New York Times* review of *Cabins*.

30. John Jacob Niles, "Doris Ulmann: As I Remember Her," *The Appalachian Photographs of Doris Ulmann* (Penland, North Carolina: The Jargon Society, 1971).

31. Niles.

32. Jonathan Williams, "They All Want to Go and Dress Up," preface to *The Appalachian Photographs of Doris Ulmann* (Penland, North Carolina: The Jargon Society, 1971).

33. Niles.

34. Reviews of *Culture in the South* were highly favorable. It was described as "authoritative," and praised for its objectivity and critical analysis of southern history and contemporary culture (Marion A. Knight, Mertice M. James, and Dorothy Brown, eds., *The Book Review Digest* Thirtieth Annual Cumulation, March 1934 to February 1935 Inclusive. New York: The H. W. Wilson Company, 1935). The fact that the majority of the book's 31 contributors were southerners made the work's objectivity especially remarkable to many reviewers. Dorothy Scarborough, writing for the *New York Times Book Review* of April 1, 1934, stated:

> This is a rich and complex book, a regional study of unusual importance. Here thirty-one Southerners ... discuss the cultural aspects of the South in a spirit of scientific investigation, holding accuracy of fact higher than tradition or prejudice. The book's sincerity is not to be questioned.... [Dorothy Scarborough, "The South: Her Level of Culture," *The New York Times Book Review* January to June 1934. New York: The New York Times and Arno Press, 1970]

Constance Rourke in the February 4, 1934, edition of *Books* wrote: "The whole volume may be construed as an effort to break up the fixed notion of a 'solid South,' and it succeeds because the many facets of a complex life are so brilliantly clarified." (Knight et al., 210)

Still, one reviewer, for the *Boston Transcript*, found the book less fulfilling. He/she wrote "[the book's] contributors certainly deserve little commendation here either for accuracy of information or for balanced judgment of opposing factors shaping a vanished civilization." (Knight et al., 210)

35. W. T. Couch, ed., *Culture in the South* (Chapel Hill: The University of North Carolina Press, 1935), 695.

36. Couch 695. In the short biographies of the book's contributors, it is stated that "For approximately twenty years [Hatcher] has given himself to the task of bringing decency and richness of life to the remote regions of Appalachia." (695) Inferring from references in his article, it is apparent that the regions of Appalachian Kentucky, Virginia, and West Virginia were the areas in which Hatcher had the most personal contact.

37. J. Wesley Hatcher, "Appalachian America," *Culture in the South* (Chapel Hill: The University of North Carolina Press, 1935), 377. Utilizing statistics from the 1930 census, he showed that there were 100,000 more farms in Appalachia than the land could bear. It was these 100,000 families (out of some 300,000 other families) that was so often the fodder of the authors who produced the popular conceptions of Appalachian America. Stripped of romanticism, here were the conditions which translated into terms of real life, told, in Hatcher's words, "a story of unbelievable tragedy." (377)

38. Hatcher 380, 381. He cited how timber and mineral rights were purchased for a song: $1 an acre, and in some instances as low as 35 cents. Moreover,

the region as a whole did not reap the benefits of taxes or royalties from the exploitation of its natural resources. Once an area was exhausted of its timber or mineral wealth, the lumber companies and mining operations often left like thieves in the night, without leaving the mountain people with any funds for roads, schools, or any other public improvements. (380)

Appalachia's most important and valuable resource—its people—were too often exploited in the region's mines, and cotton and rayon mills. The region was largely a graveyard for unions. Hatcher noted that invariably "public sentiment and the instrumentalities of government and church have given their uncompromising support to the heel which crushed [organized labor]." Without the protection of unions, Appalachia's mill and mine workers were at the mercy of predatory managers, who made them work intolerably long hours in conditions that were often inhumane, dangerous, and sometimes deadly. (381)

39. Hatcher 381. Hatcher stated:

> As is true throughout the field of human relationships and activities, there are varying levels of economic and cultural conditions, of intelligence and morality among the people of the mountains. On the basis of these differences, separated by cleavages which are deep and wide, there are distinct classes. They maintain different standards of living, speak different languages, accept different scales of values, and maintain different modes of conduct. Distances between the classes are fixed and maintained by well-established custom and definite attitudes. They live and move in different circles. Antipathy rather than sympathy characterizes the relationships among them...These facts are fundamental in the entire social fabric of this section. To neglect them is grossly misleading. [381]

40. Hatcher 382.
41. Hatcher 386.
42. Hatcher 386–387.
43. Hatcher 387.
44. Hatcher 387, 388.
45. Hatcher 387.
46. Hatcher 387.
47. Bessie Willis Hoyt, *Come When the Timber Turns* (Banner Elk, North Carolina: Pudding Stone Press, 1983), 176.
48. Hatcher 387.
49. Hatcher 388.
50. J. Russell Smith, *Men and Resources: A Study of North America and Its Place in World Geography* (New York and Chicago: Harcourt, Brace and Company, 1937), vi. Conceived within the social and economic milieu of the Great Depression, and the ecological disaster of the Dust Bowl, the book's overt goal was to show its readers "how to make full use of [North America's] resources, how to operate industries and run communities in a way that makes possible the good life." (vi)
51. Smith 147, 148. Smith stated that the region had few roads, and hence most of the residents still lived in cabins made of logs from their mountains, since they could not haul other building material in on the existing horse trails. Few

farms had any other vehicle besides a sled. Some of the residents were still partly clothed by the wool of their own sheep, which they themselves spun and wove. (147, 148)

52. Smith 148.

53. Smith 163.

54. Smith 164.

55. Hatcher 398.

56. Hatcher 399.

57. Conversation with Melvin and Regina Jones, Old Beech Mountain, North Carolina, July 1997. Melvin Jones is a Mason and deacon in the Flat Springs Baptist Church.

58. Watkins 236. "The cold North explained the working power of New Englanders while the warm climate of the South produced laziness, etc." (236)

59. Smith 132–133.

60. Batteau 200.

61. Found in Trivett's papers is an interesting piece of information which suggests that he considered his photography as art. In September 1909 Trivett received correspondence from the School of Applied Art of Battle Creek, Michigan. Only the envelope and four brief articles about the school's correspondence art courses survive, and what they reveal is tantalizingly too little. It is not known, for instance, if the school offered instruction in photography—and hence if photography was viewed by the school as an art. Nevertheless, the school guaranteed that their courses were "thoroughly PRACTICAL" and would result in "PECUNIARY RETURNS" for their students. Applicants were admonished to be brief when they wrote to the school: "*Under no circumstances send them drawings for criticism. They are busy people. All you are really entitled to ask them is this: 'Is the School of Applied Art reliable?'*" Whether or not Trivett sent an application to the school is not known.

62. Jerald Maddox, "Photography as Folk Art," *One Hundred Years of Photographic History: Essays in Honor of Beaumont Newhall* (Albuquerque, New Mexico: University of New Mexico Press, 1975), 104.

63. Charles A. Watkins, "Why Have There Been No Great Appalachian Photographers?" *Now & Then: The Appalachian Magazine* 14, no. 2 (Summer 1997): 21–25. Watkins writes:

> Certainly we will be far more successful in understanding Appalachian photography if we are willing to accept picturemen as good, solid photographic technicians instead of seeking the masters among them.... Were any of [the] picturemen great? The term is meaningless, or at least it should be if we are going to make any progress understanding these unique images. Let us say instead that they were successful and that their work outlives them. What more could any artist want? [22, 25]

64. F. Jack Hurley, *Portrait of a Decade: Roy Stryker and the Development of Documentary Photography in the Thirties*, photographic editing by Robert J. Doherty (Baton Rouge, LA: A Da Capo Paperback, 1972), 32.

65. Hurley 32.

66. William Stott, *Documentary Expression and Thirties America* (New York: Oxford University Press, 1973), 5–6.

67. Stott 12.

68. Stott 18, 21.

69. Stott 21.

70. Stott 73.

71. David Featherstone, *Doris Ulmann: American Portraits* (Albuquerque, New Mexico: University of New Mexico Press, 1985), 32–33.

72. David Moltke-Hansen, "Seeing the Highlands, 1900–1939: Southwestern Virginia Through the Lens of T. R. Phelps," *Southern Cultures* 1, no. 1 (1994): 25.

73. James Curtis, *Mind's Eye, Mind's Truth: FSA Photography Reconsidered* (Philadelphia: Temple University Press, 1989), viii. Evans was an advocate "of the single transcendent image," though in practice he often made multiple exposures of the same subject. (viii) In fact, the "shotgun method" of photography was and still is widely practiced by most professional photographers.

74. Of course, Trivett and the other picturemen always had leeway to make fine adjustments in composition and contrast in the darkroom.

75. Curtis 27.

76. Curtis 27.

77. Curtis 27.

78. Viola Ward Guy, interview by author, 17 October 1997, Old Beech Mountain, North Carolina, tape recording. Guy, a frequent sitter of Trivett's when she was growing up, recalled that Trivett would often tell his patrons how he wanted them to pose.

79. Charles H. Caffin, *Photography as a Fine Art* (New York: Doubleday, Page & Company, 1901; reprint, with an introduction by Thomas F. Barrow, Hastings-on-Hudson, New York: Morgan & Morgan, Inc., 1971), 9–10.

80. Caffin 9–10.

81. I have used the 1920 census to derive the statistics on Beech Mountain Township. For the information on Avery and Watauga counties, I have used Charles S. Johnson and Lewis W. Jones, Buford H. Junker, Eli S. Marks, and Preston Valin's *Statistical Atlas of Southern Counties: Listing and Analysis of Socio-Economic Indices of 1,104 Southern Counties* with consultants Edwin R. Embree and W. Loyd Warner (Chapel Hill: The University of North Carolina Press, 1941), which utilized information from the 1930 census.

82. Eight homes, or 5 percent, were listed as mortgaged in the 1920 census; 10 homes, or 6 percent were rented, and 23, or 13 percent were listed as "unknown."

83. Of 312 people listed as working, 226 or 72 percent were listed as farmers or farm laborers.

84. *1920 North Carolina Census: Avery County, Vol. 6: Beech Mountain Township* (Washington, D. C.: National Archives).

85. *1920 Avery Census.* There were also 3 carpenters, 2 family servants, 1 dealer in ferns, 1 dealer in furs, 1 stock farm overseer, 1 machine shop laborer, 1 laborer at a salt factory, 1 contractor for an iron mine, 1 laundress at a training school, and 2 postal workers.

86. *1920 Avery Census.*

87. *1920 Avery Census.*

88. *1920 Avery Census.* Fifteen females (33 percent of the females listed as

illiterate), were age 50 or older. Nine males (28 percent of the males listed), were over the age of 50.

89. Reconstruction politics played a part in the dearth of funds in western North Carolina from 1865 to 1881. See Ina Woestemeyer Van Noppen and John J. Van Noppen's *Western North Carolina Since the Civil War* (Boone, North Carolina: Appalachian Consortium Press, 1973), pages 121–131 for a full discussion of education (or lack thereof), in the mountains during this time.

90. Johnson et al., 178, 192.

91. The date of this photograph was determined by the birth dates of the men identified in the picture. These dates were obtained from the *Index to Vital Statistics: Births* for both Avery and Watauga counties, and by utilizing birth date information from the 1920 census of Avery County. Dudley Trivett was born ca. 1896, Leonard Story was born in 1899, and Willie Harmon was born in 1900. Judging from their appearance in the photograph, I have estimated the photo to have been taken in the 1940s. The dates of the other photographs in this chapter have been estimated in the same fashion.

92. Sheppard x, xi.

93. An ad found in the February 2, 1928, edition of the *Avery Advocate* shows that mountain people themselves often enjoyed and patronized popular caricatures of Appalachia presented in the entertainment industries. The ad proclaimed the coming of the "HILL BILLIES"—"POPULAR RADIO, PHONOGRAPH & RECORD ARTISTS" for a performance at the Cranberry High School four miles outside of Avery's county seat of Newland. The troupe was listed as presenting "Mountaineer Melodies, Vaudeville, Novelty Fiddling and Hawaiian Trio." A week later in the February 9th edition of the *Advocate*, it was reported that the "Hill Billies'" show at Cranberry High had been "enjoyed by a good crowd." (See "Hill Billies at Cranberry," front page.) One of the performers was a native of Avery County—"our own [as the paper put it] 'Spark Plug' and 'Wonder [Bear]?' Walter Hughes on the guitar, met with continued applause." Noting the widespread popularity of such "Appalachian" acts, the article concluded by stating "Many of the pieces played by these artists are those heard and enjoyed today on our best selling records."

94. Moltke-Hansen 26.

95. Troy Guy, first person on the left, was born in 1909. I estimate from the photograph that he was around 20 years old when this picture was taken.

96. Horton Cooper, *History of Avery County, North Carolina* (Asheville, North Carolina: Biltmore Press, 1964), 56–57.

97. Cooper 62.

98. Daniel J. Whitener, *Story of Watauga County: A Souvenir of Watauga Centennial* (Boone, North Carolina: Town of Boone, 1949), 49.

99. The patriotic sentiments of Avery County residents between the World Wars was explicitly expressed on the front page of the February 16, 1933, edition of the *Avery Advocate* in an article entitled "Avery County Boys Given Opportunity to Attend Military Camp." In the summers of 1932 and 1933, the federal government held "Citizens Military Training Camps (C.M.T.C.)" throughout the United States, with the intended purpose of

[training] good healthy Americans [17–18 years old] to carry on the Nation's work and perpetuate its institutions; [to] develop young men who will hold their heads high and take honored places in the community and who will spread the doctrine of healthy, democratic Americanism by their daily lives.

The paper referred to the opportunity to attend one of the North Carolina camps as "the Government's splendid offer." To apply, the young men had to have a physical examination, vaccinations against small pox and typhoid fever, and, perhaps most importantly, "a certificate of good moral character." In 1932 two young men from Avery County, Frank Buchanan of Newland and Ernest C. Franklin of Altamont, were selected to attend the C.M.T. Camp at Fort Bragg. The paper invited 1933 applicants to "ask any of them what they think of it and get first hand information." The article closed by exhorting Avery County "boys" to get their applications in early—before March 15.

100. See page 28 of Dan Crowe's *Old Butler and Watauga Academy* (Elizabethton, Tennessee: Dan Crowe, 1983).

101. Hal L. Cohen, ed., *1922 Montgomery Ward Catalog* reprinted in its original form with introduction by Robert E. Brooker, Chairman of the Board—Montgomery Ward, and Louis Sobol (HC Publishers Inc., 1969), 5. The opening page of the women's clothing section stated: "Montgomery Ward's Fashion Rooms in New York are the scene of our story. Our own Fashion Experts are at work making their selections for this catalogue." (5)

102. Cohen 5.

103. Haskell Trivett once showed me the very same banjo in the picture. It was made with stretched groundhog hide. He said that Willie had made the banjo and could play it quite well.

104. W. R. Trivett's son, Haskell, can be seen tenth from the left in the front row of children in the picture. He appears to be around 10 years old, hence the date of the photograph being around 1928–29.

105. Watkins, "Why Have There Been No Great Appalachian Photographers," 25. He asserts that the pens and pencils in the men's coat pockets were visual cues of the sitters' ability to read and write.

106. That many of the mountain people photographed by Trivett viewed nature (and hence their rural surroundings) favorably is further evidenced by Trivett's use of painted backdrops—both of which depicted (however roughly) natural settings. See plate 89 for one of the painted landscape backdrops frequently used by Trivett. He would have not used these particular backdrops if he knew that they would not be pleasing to large numbers of his patrons.

Postscript. The Watauga Democrat and Avery Advocate

1. Whitener 48.

2. See "Anarchy the New Peril," *Watauga Democrat*, 16 May 1912, p. 1 and "Ocotal Battlefield and Its Two Heroes," *Avery Advocate*, 1 September 1927, p. 1. What made the *Democrat*'s report so disturbing was that the May Day meeting had been infiltrated by Wobblies—members of the Industrial Workers of the World, who nearly started a riot by tearing down a U.S. flag on the stand where

speakers from the Socialist Party were going to speak. The concerned author of the article concluded that the nation was headed for "the rankest anarchy."

The *Advocate* featured a photograph of two U. S. soldiers superimposed over an aerial photograph of Ocotal, Nicaragua. Ocotal had been the scene of a 17-hour battle between Nicaraguan rebel forces led by General Sandino and U.S. backed government troops. The Sandino rebels were repulsed from the town with the aid of U.S. bombing planes; the two soldiers featured in the photograph had been cited for the Distinguished Service medal for their actions in the battle.

3. Edward W. Pickard, "News Review of Current Events: Champion Tanney Defeats Dempsey in Lively Ten-Round Battle," *Avery Advocate*, 6 October 1927, p. 1.

4. For news about the First World War, see "The Crime of the Century," and also "Belgians Kill Thousands When Germans Attack Fort," *Watauga Democrat*, 13 August 1914, p. 1.

5. An ad for "Ford Cars, Reo Cars, Hudson Cars," featured in the July 6, 1916, edition of the *Watauga Democrat* was for a dealership in Lenoir and North Wilkesboro, North Carolina. See also "Automobile Passenger Service," *Watauga Democrat*, 6 July 1916. By 1919 mountain residents could purchase a Ford from the Watauga Motor Company of Boone; by the late 1920s the P. & P. Chevrolet Company of Newland was offering GM products of sale. "Watauga Motor Company," *Watauga Democrat*, 13 November, and "P. & P. Chevrolet Company," *Avery Advocate*, 2 August 1928.

6. "Delco Light," *Watauga Democrat*, 27 November 1919.

7. "Washing Machines and How to Make a Wise Selection," *Avery Advocate*, 13 October 1927.

8. The Brinkley ad emphasized the newness and modernity of his stock: "My store is rapidly being filled up again with new and stylish goods.... Everything the Ladies and children need is here for you in fresh, up-to-date goods."

9. In November 1928 the Elk Park Picture Show also received election returns via radio which they broadcasted through their loudspeaker from 1:00 P.M. "until the fun [was] over." Also showing that November was the First National movie *Patent Leather Kid*. "Election Returns, Elk Park Picture Show," *Avery Advocate*, 1 November 1928.

10. The reporter noted that Morris would not discuss "wimmen."

11. "Cranberry Girls Champions of the South," *Avery Advocate*, 28 March 1929, p. 1.

12. In the article the word "peers" was misprinted as "pers." The *Advocate* was plagued with such gaffes throughout its publication.

13. "Cranberry Champions" 1.

Sources Consulted

Unpublished and Private Papers

Minutes of the Flat Springs Baptist Church of Christ Book I—1902–1937, and Book II—1938–1973. Melvin and Regina Jones, Old Beech Mountain, North Carolina.

W. R. Trivett papers [photocopy]. In the possession of the author by permission of Susie Guy Trivett, Flat Springs, North Carolina.

Interviews

Greene, Ottie, best friend of Haskell Trivett, W. R. Trivett's son. Interview by author, 21 July 1996, Flat Springs, North Carolina. A tape recording is in the possession of the author.

Guy, Viola Ward. Interview by author, 17 October 1997, Flat Springs, North Carolina. A tape recording is in the possession of the author.

Trivett, Auborn W., W. R. Trivett's nephew. Interview by author, 16 July 1996, Sugar Grove, North Carolina. A tape recording is in the possession of the author.

Trivett, Susie Guy, W. R. Trivett's daughter-in-law. Interview by author, 22 June 1995, Flat Springs, North Carolina. A tape recording is in the possession of the author.

Dissertations and Theses

Bingham, Paul W. "The Growth and Development of Education in Watauga County." Master's thesis, Appalachian State Teacher's College, 1950.

Newspapers

Avery Advocate 1927–1937.
Avery Journal 11 August 1966.
Watauga Democrat 1914–1937.

Government Publications and Records

Avery County Book of Deeds Book 10 and Book 20. Newland, North Carolina: Avery County Courthouse, Register of Deeds.

Index to Marriages from 1873–1974 L–Z, Watauga County. Boone, North Carolina: Watauga County Courthouse, Register of Deeds.

Index to Vital Statistics: Births, Avery County. Newland, North Carolina: Avery County Courthouse, Register of Deeds.

Index to Vital Statistics: Births, Watauga County. Boone, North Carolina: Watauga County Courthouse, Register of Deeds.

Index to Vital Statistics: Deaths A–Z, Watauga County. Boone, North Carolina: Watauga County Courthouse, Register of Deeds.

The National Archives and National Archives and Records Service, General Services Administration. *Selected Records of the National Youth Administration Relating to North Carolina 1935–1943* Record Group 119. Records of the National Youth Administration, Washington, D.C.: The National Archives, 1984. Microfilm.

1920 North Carolina Census: Avery County, Vol. 6: Beech Mountain Township. Washington, D.C.: National Archives.

Vital Statistics: Delayed Births, Watauga County vol. 9. Boone, North Carolina: Watauga County Courthouse, Register of Deeds.

Books and Articles

Arthur, John Preston. *Western North Carolina: A History 1730–1913*. Raleigh, North Carolina: Edwards & Broughton Printing Company, 1914; reprint, Spartanburg, South Carolina: The Reprint Company, 1973.

Batteau, Allen W. *The Invention of Appalachia*. Tuscon: The University of Arizona Press, 1990.

Caffin, Charles H. *Photography as a Fine Art*. New York: Doubleday, Page, 1901; reprint, with an introduction by Thomas F. Barrow, Hastings-on-Hudson, New York: Morgan & Morgan, Inc., 1971.

Cohen, Hal L., ed. *1922 Montgomery Ward Catalog*. Reprinted in its original form with introduction by Robert E. Brooker, Chairman of the Board—Montomery Ward, and Louis Sobol. HC Publishers Inc., 1969.

Cooper, Horton. *History of Avery County, North Carolina*. Asheville, North Carolina: Biltmore Press, 1964.

Couch, W. T., ed. *Culture in the South*. Chapel Hill: The University of North Carolina Press, 1935.

Crowe, Dan. *Old Butler and Watauga Academy*. Elizabethton, Tennessee: By the author, 1983.

Curtis, James. *Mind's Eye, Mind's Truth: FSA Photography Reconsidered*. Philadelphia: Temple University Press, 1989.

Featherstone, David. *Doris Ulmann: American Portraits*. Albuquerque: University of New Mexico Press, 1985.

The Focal Encyclopedia of Photography. New York: Macmillan, 1960.

Gaffney, Sana Ross, et al. *The Heritage of Watauga County, North Carolina* vol. 1. Winston-Salem, North Carolina: Heritage of Watauga County Book Committee in cooperation with the History Division of Hunter Publishing Company, 1984.

Gernsheim, Helmut, and Allison Gernsheim. *The History of Photography from the Earliest Use of the Camera Obscura in the Eleventh Century Up to 1914.* London, New York, Toronto: Geoffrey Cumberlege, Oxford University Press, 1955.

Harmon, Terry L. *The Harmon Family 1670–1984: The Genealogy of Cutliff Harmon and His Descendants* vol. 1. Boone, North Carolina: By the author, 1984.

Hatcher, J. Wesley. "Appalachian America." *Culture in the South.* Chapel Hill: The University of North Carolina Press, 1935.

Hawthorne, Ann, ed. *The Picture Man.* Photographs by Paul Buchanan, with foreword and introduction by Bruce Morton. Chapel Hill: The University of North Carolina Press, 1993.

Hoyt, Bessie Willis. *Come When the Timber Turns.* Banner Elk, North Carolina: Pudding Stone Press, 1983.

Hurley, F. Jack. *Portrait of a Decade: Roy Stryker and the Development of Documentary Photography in the Thirties.* Photographic editing by Robert J. Doherty. Baton Rouge, Louisiana: A Da Capo Paperback, 1972.

Isbell, Robert. *The Last Chivaree: The Hicks Family of Beech Mountain.* Foreword by Wilma Dykeman. Chapel Hill: The University of North Carolina Press, 1996.

James, Mertice M., and Dorothy Brown, eds. *The Book Review Digest: Thirty-First Annual Cumulation, March 1935 to February 1936 Inclusive.* New York: H. W. Wilson, 1936.

Johnson, Charles S., et al. *Statistical Atlas of Southern Counties: Listing and Analysis of Socio Economic Indices of 1,104 Southern Counties.* With consultants Edwin R. Embree and W. Loyd Warner. Chapel Hill: The University of North Carolina Press, 1941.

Knight, Marion A., Mertice M. James, and Dorothy Brown, eds. *The Book Review Digest: Thirtieth Annual Cumulation, March 1934 to February 1935 Inclusive.* New York: H. W. Wilson, 1935.

Maddox, Jerald. "Photography as Folk Art." *One Hundred Years of Photographic History: Essays in Honor of Beaumont Newhall.* Albuquerque: University of New Mexico Press, 1975.

Moltke-Hansen, David. "Seeing the Highlands, 1900–1939: Southwestern Virginia Through the Lens of T. R. Phelps." *Southern Cultures* 1 (1994): 23–49.

Newhall, Beaumont. *The History of Photography from 1839 to the Present Day.* New York: The Museum of Modern Art, 1949.

Niles, John Jacob. "Doris Ulmann: As I Remember Her." *The Appalachian Photographs of Doris Ulmann.* Penland, North Carolina: The Jargon Society, 1971.

Ross, Carl A., Jr., ed. *The 1870 Census of Watauga County, North Carolina.* Boone, North Carolina: Department of History, Appalachian State University, 1982.

___. *The 1880 Census of Watauga County, North Carolina.* Boone, North Carolina: Department of History, Appalachian State University, 1983.

___. *The 1900 Census of Watauga County, North Carolina* vol. 2. Boone, North Carolina: Department of History, Appalachian State University, 1984.

___. *The 1910 Census of Watauga County, North Carolina* vol. 2. Boone, North Carolina: Department of History, Appalachian State University, 1986.

Scarborough, Dorothy. "The South: Her Level of Culture." *The New York Times Book Review* January to June 1934. New York: The New York Times and Arno Press, 1970.

Shapiro, Henry D. *Appalachia on Our Mind: The Southern Mountains and Mountaineers in the American Consciousness, 1870–1920*. Chapel Hill: The University of North Carolina Press, 1978.

Sheppard, Muriel Early. *Cabins in the Laurel*. Foreword by John Ehle, 1991 ed. Chapel Hill: The University of North Carolina Press, 1935, 1991.

Shoemake, Reka W., and others. *Development of Public Education in Watauga County, North Carolina* compiled by a Bicentennial committee. Boone, North Carolina: Appalachian State University, 1976.

Smith, J. Russell. *Men and Resources: A Study of North America and Its Place in World Geography*. New York and Chicago: Harcourt, Brace and Company, 1937.

Stott, William. *Documentary Expression and Thirties America*. New York: Oxford University Press, 1973.

Szarkowski, John. *Photography Until Now*. New York, Boston, Toronto: The Museum of Modern Art, 1989.

Van Noppen, Ina Woestemeyer, and John J. Van Noppen. *Western North Carolina Since the Civil War*. Boone, North Carolina: Appalachian Consortium Press, 1973.

Watkins, Charles Alan. "Merchandising the Mountaineer: Photography, the Great Depression, and *Cabins in the Laurel*." *Appalachian Journal: A Regional Studies Review* (Spring 1985): 215–238.

___. "Why Have There Been No Great Appalachian Photographers?" *Now & Then: The Appalachian Magazine* 14 (Summer 1997): 21–25.

Welling, William. *Photography in America: The Formative Years 1839–1900*. New York: Thomas Y. Crowell Company, 1978.

Whitener, Daniel J. *Story of Watauga County: A Souvenir of Watauga Centennial*. Boone, North Carolina: Town of Boone, 1949.

Williams, Jonathan. "They All Want to Go and Dress Up." *The Appalachian Photographs of Doris Ulmann*. Penland, North Carolina: The Jargon Society, 1971.

Index